BOOKBINDING
as a
HANDCRAFT

By MANLY BANISTER
Photographs and Drawings by the Author

 STERLING PUBLISHING CO., INC.   NEW YORK

This book is dedicated to the memory of
MR. ANSON HERRICK
of San Francisco, friend, amateur bookbinder, gentleman.

First paperback printing 1986

Copyright © 1975 by Sterling Publishing Co., Inc.
Two Park Avenue, New York, N.Y. 10016
Distributed in Australia by Capricorn Book Co. Pty. Ltd.
Unit 5C1 Lincoln St., Lane Cove, N.S.W. 2066
Distributed in the United Kingdom by Blandford Press
Link House, West Street, Poole, Dorset BH15 1LL, England
Distributed in Canada by Oak Tree Press Ltd.
% Canadian Manda Group, P.O. Box 920, Station U
Toronto, Ontario, Canada M8Z 5P9
Manufactured in the United States of America
All rights reserved
Library of Congress Catalog Card No.: 75-14522
Sterling ISBN 0-8069-6352-2 Paper

Contents

BOOKBINDING STEP BY STEP

**BOOKS & MAGAZINES
WITH FOLDED SECTIONS**

**PAPERBACKS, MANUSCRIPTS
AND OTHER PUBLICATIONS
COMPOSED OF SINGLE SHEETS**

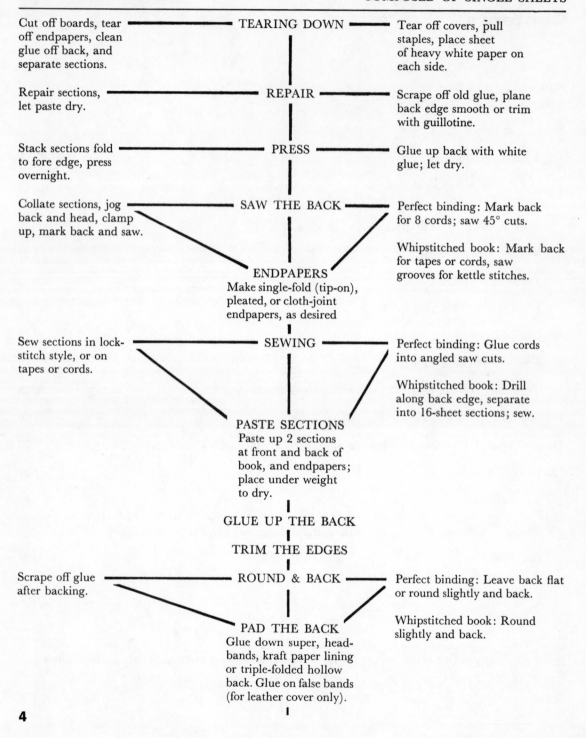

TEARING DOWN

Cut off boards, tear off endpapers, clean glue off back, and separate sections.

Tear off covers, pull staples, place sheet of heavy white paper on each side.

REPAIR

Repair sections, let paste dry.

Scrape off old glue, plane back edge smooth or trim with guillotine.

PRESS

Stack sections fold to fore edge, press overnight.

Glue up back with white glue; let dry.

SAW THE BACK

Collate sections, jog back and head, clamp up, mark back and saw.

Perfect binding: Mark back for 8 cords; saw 45° cuts.

Whipstitched book: Mark back for tapes or cords, saw grooves for kettle stitches.

ENDPAPERS
Make single-fold (tip-on), pleated, or cloth-joint endpapers, as desired

SEWING

Sew sections in lock-stitch style, or on tapes or cords.

Perfect binding: Glue cords into angled saw cuts.

Whipstitched book: Drill along back edge, separate into 16-sheet sections; sew.

PASTE SECTIONS
Paste up 2 sections at front and back of book, and endpapers; place under weight to dry.

GLUE UP THE BACK

TRIM THE EDGES

ROUND & BACK

Scrape off glue after backing.

Perfect binding: Leave back flat or round slightly and back.

Whipstitched book: Round slightly and back.

PAD THE BACK
Glue down super, head-bands, kraft paper lining or triple-folded hollow back. Glue on false bands (for leather cover only).

(continued)

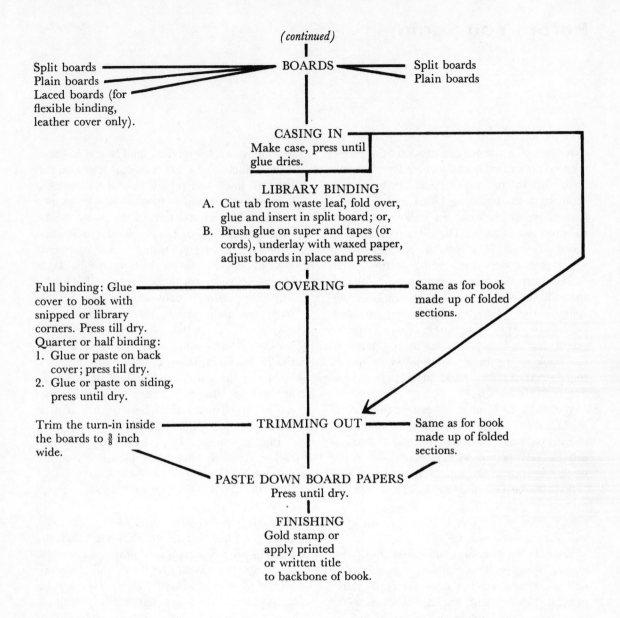

Split boards ────── BOARDS ────── Split boards
Plain boards   Plain boards
Laced boards (for
flexible binding,
leather cover only).

CASING IN
Make case, press until
glue dries.

LIBRARY BINDING
A. Cut tab from waste leaf, fold over,
   glue and insert in split board; or,
B. Brush glue on super and tapes (or
   cords), underlay with waxed paper,
   adjust boards in place and press.

Full binding: Glue ────── COVERING ────── Same as for book
cover to book with   made up of folded
snipped or library   sections.
corners. Press till dry.
Quarter or half binding:
1. Glue or paste on back
   cover; press till dry.
2. Glue or paste on siding,
   press until dry.

Trim the turn-in inside ────── TRIMMING OUT ────── Same as for book
the boards to $\frac{3}{8}$ inch   made up of folded
wide.   sections.

PASTE DOWN BOARD PAPERS
Press until dry.

FINISHING
Gold stamp or
apply printed
or written title
to backbone of book.

U.S. Measures and Metric Equivalents

$\frac{1}{8}$ inch = 3.18 millimetres	$\frac{5}{8}$ inch = 15.88 millimetres	$1\frac{1}{2}$ inch = 38.10 millimetres
$\frac{1}{4}$ inch = 6.35 millimetres	$\frac{3}{4}$ inch = 19.05 millimetres	2 inches = 50.80 millimetres
$\frac{3}{8}$ inch = 9.53 millimetres	$\frac{7}{8}$ inch = 22.23 millimetres	1 foot = 30.48 centimetres
$\frac{1}{2}$ inch = 12.70 millimetres	1 inch = 25.40 millimetres	1 yard = 0.9144 metre
	10 millimetres = 1 centimetre	

Before You Begin

Along about the 4th century A.D., the people who manufactured books—which were actually scrolls up to that time—began to turn their thoughts toward making books easier to read and to use in research, less bulky, and easier to store on shelves. The idea occurred to somebody that if sheets of parchment—on which books were then being written—were folded down the middle and sewed to thongs through the fold, the result would be something entirely new in the history of book publishing. After that, all that was required was a pair of heavy wooden boards, laced to the book at the back and hooked or locked together at the fore edge, to keep the pages flat and safe from harm.

Within a few hundred years, the art of bookbinding became fully developed and is carried on today with little difference from its origins, save that nowadays machines do the work that used to be done by human hands.

So why bookbinding by hand? There are numerous reasons. The most satisfying feeling comes from performing such a difficult craft well. Try it—you will see.

Your favorite books will wear out, and many, being both useful and valuable, you will want repaired and even rebound. Commercial binders will not do this work for you—they only bind in quantities of 100 or more copies. So, you must do it yourself.

Magazines are a form of book that arrives piecemeal, by the month. Six months' issue, or a year's issue, is designated as a volume. Some magazines are valuable enough for reference, and printed on good enough paper, so that it is worthwhile for you to bind them into permanent books.

Books published by Dover Publications, Inc., for example, are printed on good paper folded into signatures, or sections, and bound in paper covers. Such books, purchased at low cost, can be torn down and rebuilt into as handsome a volume as you want to make it. The same may be said for certain foreign language books, which are printed on paper folded into sections.

Beware, however, of trying to bind every type of book. Take care in choosing the books or magazines you want to bind or rebind. There is little use putting a book or magazine printed on cheap, pulp paper into hard covers. The covers will far outlast the book. Also, many books and magazines are printed with practically no margins—at least, the margins, including the gutter (the margin at the spine or back of the book), are so narrow that rebinding is impractical because no room is left for trimming the edges.

Illus. 25 (page 17) shows a heap of publications, such as have been discussed, that are suitable for binding.

In the following chapters, various "styles" of binding are described and demonstrated in photographs. Actually, there is no such thing as a complete "style" of binding, and the binding process is composed of numerous steps, or things that have to be done, and these can be shifted around at will. You may sew a book in any one of the ways that will be described, you may provide it with whatever style of endpapers appeals to you, and you can board it in one of the several ways described, and cover it with a wide choice of materials: paper, cloth, buckram, artificial leather, canvas, leather—and these in a wide variety of colors and surface appearance.

The amateur bookbinder has it better than the professional, in that he can pick and choose among processes and materials as it pleases him. The professional must limit him-

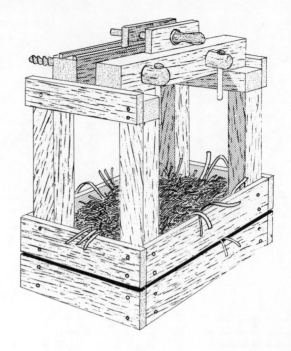

self to those materials and activities that will give him a profit for his work, when the result of it has been priced at current market value.

The bookbinder as an artist is something else again, for his real work just begins when the work of binding the book is finished. The art of decorating the spine and covers of a book has almost disappeared, except for a few practitioners. Applying gilded decoration with hand stamps is a long and tedious process, not to mention the art of designing the decoration to begin with. We shall concern ourselves only with the simplest of titling and decoration— for, with this much to start on, you can carry your activities in this field as far forward as you wish, or as it is possible for you to go.

In the styles described in the following chapters, many steps are identical with work described in a preceding chapter. In such case, instructions will not be repeated, but reference will be made to the chapter, page or illustration where the necessary information may be found.

Illus. 2—The home-made screw press is the amateur bookbinder's replacement of the all-steel letter press or nipping press.

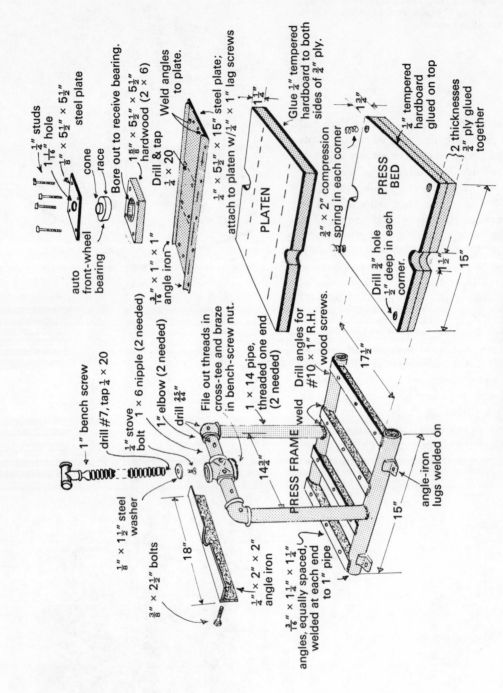

Illus. 3—Construction details of the screw press.

$\frac{1}{4}$" studs

$1\frac{1}{16}$" hole

$5\frac{1}{2}$" × $5\frac{1}{2}$" steel plate

$\frac{1}{8}$" × $5\frac{1}{2}$" × $5\frac{1}{2}$"

cone

race

Bore out to receive bearing.

Weld angles to plate.

$1\frac{5}{8}$" × $5\frac{1}{2}$" × $5\frac{1}{2}$" hardwood (2 × 6)

Drill & tap $\frac{1}{4}$ × 20

auto front-wheel bearing

$\frac{3}{16}$" × 1" × 1" angle iron

Glue $\frac{1}{4}$" tempered hardboard to both sides of $\frac{3}{4}$" ply.

$1\frac{1}{4}$"

$\frac{1}{4}$" × $5\frac{1}{2}$" × 15" steel plate; attach to platen w/$\frac{1}{4}$" × 1" lag screws

PLATEN

$\frac{3}{4}$" × 2" compression spring in each corner

$\frac{1}{4}$" tempered hardboard glued on top

$\frac{1}{3}$"

PRESS BED

2 thicknesses $\frac{3}{4}$" ply glued together

Drill $\frac{3}{4}$" hole $\frac{1}{2}$" deep in each corner.

$1\frac{1}{2}$"

15"

1" bench screw

drill #7, tap $\frac{1}{4}$ × 20

$\frac{1}{4}$" stove bolt

1" elbow (2 needed)

1" × 6 nipple (2 needed)

drill $\frac{25}{64}$"

File out threads in cross-tee and braze in bench-screw nut.

1 × 14 pipe, threaded one end (2 needed)

Drill angles for #10 × 1" R.H. wood screws.

weld

PRESS FRAME

$17\frac{1}{2}$"

$\frac{1}{8}$" × $1\frac{1}{2}$" steel washer

$\frac{3}{8}$" × $2\frac{1}{2}$" bolts

18"

$\frac{3}{16}$" × $1\frac{1}{4}$" × $1\frac{1}{4}$" angles, equally spaced, welded at each end to 1" pipe

$\frac{1}{4}$" × 2" × 2" angle iron

$14\frac{3}{4}$"

15"

angle-iron lugs welded on

1. Tools and Adhesives

What tools do you really need? To start your bookbinding "career," you need a lying press and plow with backing boards and some kind of a simple book press (Illus. 4 and 13–14). You can buy such tools ready-made (see list of suppliers on page 159), or you can make them yourself, or have them made from the drawings provided. You do not need a wide outlay of such tools as knives and hammers. If you have them, use them. Otherwise, make do with what you have.

Present-day availability of the Redibolt (threaded rod) has vastly simplified the home-shop construction of bookbinding equipment. Redibolts up to $\frac{3}{4}''$ diameter by 3 feet in length are available in hardware stores. (In metric countries, threaded rods are sold by millimetre lengths.) Larger sizes can be purchased from

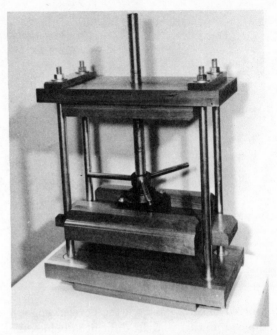

Illus. 5—The standing press. This one was made by the author from maple planks, using a 1½-inch Redibolt (threaded rod) for a press screw. It is an ideal press for the classroom or advanced amateur.

an industrial hardware dealer. Sizes up to 1½-inch diameter come in 3-foot lengths. Redibolts of 2-inch diameter and up come in 12-foot lengths, but these are larger than needed and are not to be considered. Purchase nuts required for the size of rod at the same time you buy the Redibolts.

LYING PRESS AND PLOW. (Illus. 7–8). As a lying press only, it is used to hold the book in various forwarding operations (forwarding = all the steps involved in bookbinding from tearing down the book up to but not including finishing or titling).

With the plow, it is used to trim the edges of books. With backing boards, it becomes a backing press. Note the backing boards in Illus. 8. Old-time bookbinders used boards that

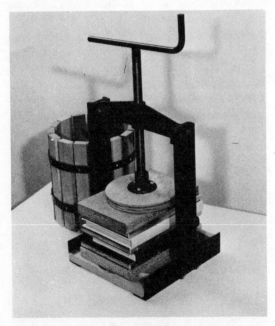

Illus. 4—A fruit press makes a good book press. The fruit cage is not used—it is present in the photo for identification only.

Illus. 6—Construction details, the standing press.

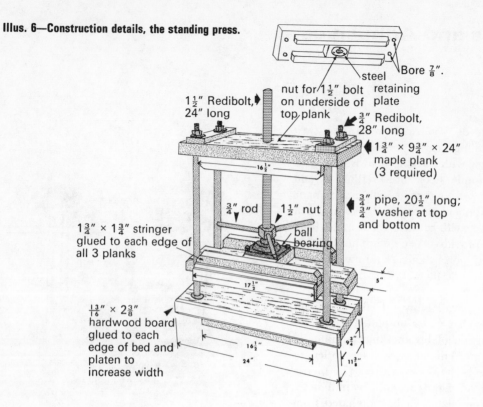

Bore $\frac{7}{8}$".

steel retaining plate

nut for $1\frac{1}{2}$" bolt on underside of top plank

$1\frac{1}{2}$" Redibolt, 24" long

$\frac{3}{4}$" Redibolt, 28" long

$1\frac{3}{4}$" × $9\frac{3}{4}$" × 24" maple plank (3 required)

16½"

$\frac{3}{4}$" rod

$1\frac{1}{2}$" nut

$\frac{3}{4}$" pipe, $20\frac{1}{2}$" long; $\frac{3}{4}$" washer at top and bottom

$1\frac{3}{4}$" × $1\frac{3}{4}$" stringer glued to each edge of all 3 planks

ball bearing

$\frac{13}{16}$" × $2\frac{3}{8}$" hardwood board glued to each edge of bed and platen to increase width

17½"

5"

16½"

24"

$9\frac{3}{4}$"

$11\frac{3}{4}$"

tapered in thickness from the beveled edge to the bottom edge and are difficult to hold while adjusting the book in the press. The boards shown rest on the tub and cannot fall through. Instead of tapering the thickness, strips of ⅛-inch hardboard are glued to the sides at the height of the cheek of the press. The purpose of these strips is the same as that of tapering the boards—to bring the pressure of the press to bear only against the line of backing and not against the entire book. Otherwise, boards narrower than the book would mark an unsightly crease across the endpapers.

Maple is recommended for all construction, but other hardwoods, where available, may be used: birch, beech, cherry, etc.

To adapt the plane blade to the plow, the areas to be drilled and cut must first be heated cherry red with a torch or in a gas flame and

allowed to cool slowly in the air. The blade can then be drilled and sawed, after which it is again heated cherry red and plunged into water to harden. To temper, place in a kitchen oven at 300° F. (148° C.) for one hour, then quench again in water.

PRESSING BOARDS. (Illus. 2 and 14). Plain pressing boards and grooving boards (to make the French groove at the hinge of the book) are needed. Plain pressing boards can be

Illus. 7—A home-made lying press and plow on its modern adaptation of the "tub."

simply pieces of plywood faced with un-tempered hardboard. If $\frac{1}{8}'' \times \frac{3}{4}''$ strip aluminum is used for the grooving jaw, the edges must be planed down to $\frac{1}{16}$-inch thick and rounded. A Surform plane does the job, followed by filing. Less work is involved if you use a $\frac{1}{16}$-inch-thick aluminum strip.

Plain pressing boards can be used instead of grooving boards for forming the French groove if *bronze* (not steel) welding rod is laid in both grooves and taped together at the ends (Illus. 235, page 136). Get $\frac{3}{32}''$ rod at your local welding supply house.

SAWING AND GLUEING CLAMP. (Illus. 11–12). A $\frac{1}{2}$-inch Redibolt is cut to size for the screws. Rivet a $\frac{1}{2}$-inch nut on one end for a head, or drill and tap one face of the nut for a $\frac{1}{4}$–20,

hollow-head set screw. Sink the nut head into the wood to keep the bolt from turning when the wing nut is tightened.

THE BOOK PRESS. (Illus. 13–14). Make one of maple, or of plywood faced with hardboard. The press screws are $\frac{1}{2}$-inch Redibolt cut to length and furnished with washers and wing nuts.

If $\frac{1}{8}$-inch strip aluminum is used for grooving jaws, hand-plane the edge with a Surform plane and file to shape—or simply use $\frac{1}{16}$-inch

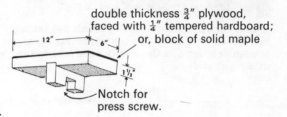

double thickness $\frac{3}{4}''$ plywood, faced with $\frac{1}{4}''$ tempered hardboard; or, block of solid maple

12″   6″   1½″

Notch for press screw.

Illus. 8—Construction details of the press and plow.

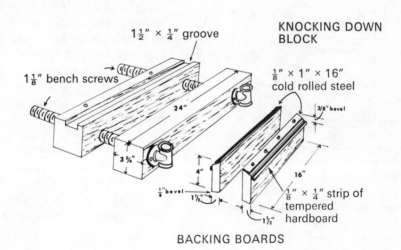

$1\frac{1}{2}'' \times \frac{1}{4}''$ groove

$1\frac{1}{8}''$ bench screws

KNOCKING DOWN BLOCK

$\frac{1}{8}'' \times 1'' \times 16''$ cold rolled steel

24″

3/8″ bevel

3¾″

4″

16″

$\frac{1}{8}''$ bevel   1½″

$\frac{1}{8}'' \times \frac{1}{4}''$ strip of tempered hardboard

1½″

BACKING BOARDS

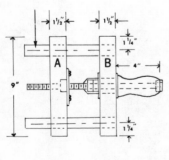

1½″   1½″

1¼″

A   B   4″

9″

1¼″

PLOW—TOP VIEW

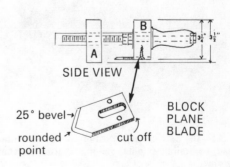

B

A   3¼″   3½″

SIDE VIEW

25° bevel

rounded point

cut off

BLOCK PLANE BLADE

11

Illus. 9—Lying press with backing boards and backing hammer. An electric hot plate is handy for heating glue in a double boiler, as well as for type and ornaments in titling with gold.

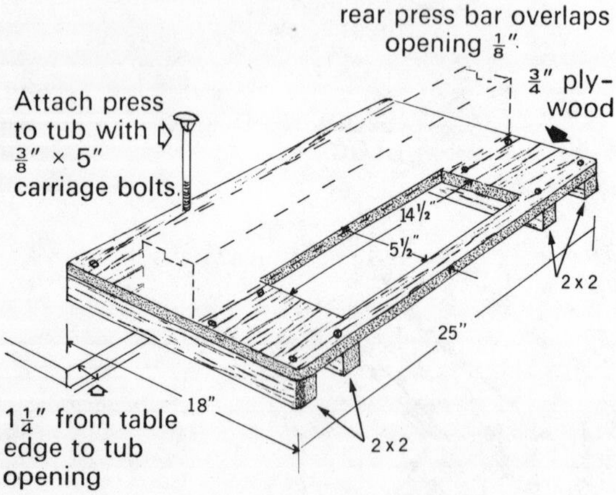

rear press bar overlaps opening ⅛"

Attach press to tub with ⅜" × 5" carriage bolts.

¾" plywood

14½"

5½"

2 x 2

25"

18"

2 x 2

1¼" from table edge to tub opening

Illus. 10—Construction details of the press tub.

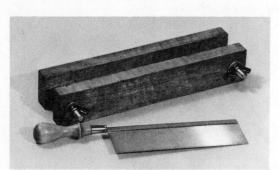

Illus. 11—The sawing and glueing clamp with fine-toothed, dovetail saw to be used in preparing the book for sewing.

12

strip aluminum. Steel jaws can be ground on a carborundum wheel and the edges rounded with a file.

SEWING EQUIPMENT. (Illus. 15–16). The sewing frame is simplest to make. Tapes or cords are held by thumb-tacks (drawing pins) for sewing books. The sewing table, or sewing press, may be provided with short screws as shown, or equipped with long Redibolt screws so that a number of books can be sewed one after the other without cutting down.

Tape keys hold the tape at the bottom; cord keys are used to hold cords. Their use will be explained later.

STABBING CLAMP. Use of this device is explained in Chapter 13 where sewing books made up of single sheets is undertaken.

BENCH PRESS. (Illus. 19–20). A luxury for the advanced amateur, a necessity for the classroom. All operations conducted with the lying press, except trimming the book, can also be performed with a bench press. The use of large Redibolts for press screws is recommended, since these are threaded with the National Coarse Series of threads (formerly U.S. Standard). The following table shows the relationship between screw diameter and number of threads per inch:

½ inch—13 threads per inch
¾ inch—10 threads per inch
1 inch— 8 threads per inch
1¼ inch— 7 threads per inch
1½ inch— 6 threads per inch

(See metric table on page 5 for conversions.)

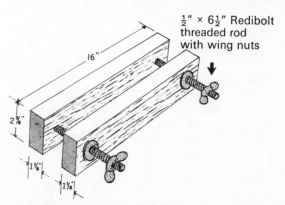

½" × 6½" Redibolt threaded rod with wing nuts

16"

2⅜"

1⅛"

1⅛"

Illus. 12—Sawing and glueing clamp.

Illus. 13—Simple book presses. (Left) Plywood, reinforced with oak flooring strips. (Right) Solid maple, $1\frac{1}{8}" \times 9\frac{3}{4}" \times 16"$.

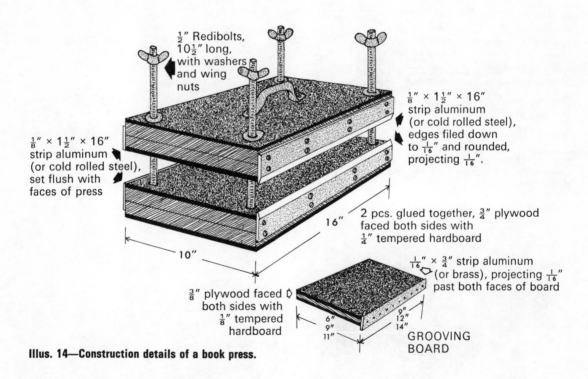

$\frac{1}{2}"$ Redibolts, $10\frac{1}{2}"$ long, with washers and wing nuts

$\frac{1}{8}" \times 1\frac{1}{2}" \times 16"$ strip aluminum (or cold rolled steel), edges filed down to $\frac{1}{16}"$ and rounded, projecting $\frac{1}{16}"$.

$\frac{1}{8}" \times 1\frac{1}{2}" \times 16"$ strip aluminum (or cold rolled steel), set flush with faces of press

2 pcs. glued together, $\frac{3}{4}"$ plywood faced both sides with $\frac{1}{4}"$ tempered hardboard

16"

10"

$\frac{3}{8}"$ plywood faced both sides with $\frac{1}{8}"$ tempered hardboard

$\frac{1}{16}" \times \frac{3}{4}"$ strip aluminum (or brass), projecting $\frac{1}{16}"$ past both faces of board

6"
9"
9"
12"
11"
14"

GROOVING BOARD

Illus. 14—Construction details of a book press.

The sloped (45° angle) faces cut into the press bars are sawed out with a bandsaw, then sanded and smoothed by hand. These provide room for using the backing hammer, stamping tools, and so on.

THE SCREW PRESS. (Illus. 2–3 and 4). Useful for pressing books and as a printing press for printing titles on paper, to be pasted to the back of the book.

THE STANDING PRESS. (Illus. 5–6). The

13

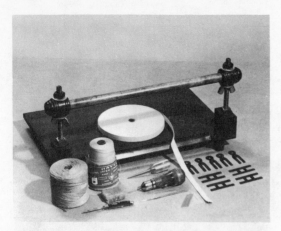

Illus. 15—The sewing table. Accessories: tape keys, cord keys, roll of sewing tape, sewing cord, unbleached linen thread, needles, beeswax, awl, stitching device for sewing single sheets (optional), #11 crochet hook.

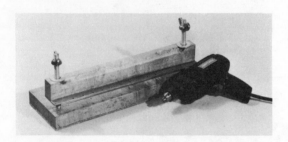

Illus. 17—Stabbing clamp with quarter-inch, variable speed drill for stabbing (drilling) books made up of single sheets.

Illus. 19—Bench presses (also called finishing presses). Press at left rear is made of 3¾-inch square cherry—miniature "tub" holds press above table surface. Press at right front is made of 1 × 3 fir (deal) glue-laminated, faced on edge-sides with tempered hardboard. For press screws, a ¾-inch Redibolt was cut in two.

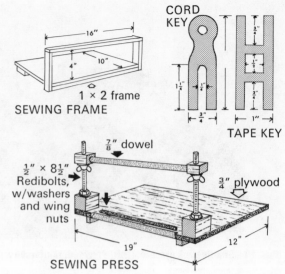

CORD KEY

1 × 2 frame

SEWING FRAME

TAPE KEY

⅞" dowel

½" × 8½" Redibolts, w/washers and wing nuts

¾" plywood

19"

12"

SEWING PRESS

Illus. 16—Sewing equipment.

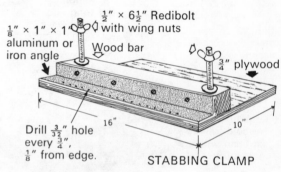

½" × 6½" Redibolt with wing nuts

⅛" × 1" × 1" aluminum or iron angle

Wood bar

¾" plywood

Drill ³⁄₃₂" hole every ¾", ⅛" from edge.

16"

10"

STABBING CLAMP

Illus. 18—Stabbing clamp.

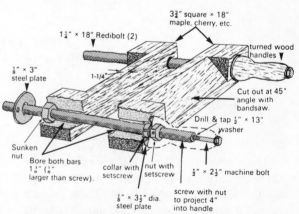

3¾" square × 18" maple, cherry, etc.

1¼" × 18" Redibolt (2)

turned wood handles

⅛" × 3" steel plate

1-1/4"

Cut out at 45° angle with bandsaw.

Drill & tap ½" × 13"

washer

Sunken nut

Bore both bars 1¹⁄₈" (⅛" larger than screw).

collar with setscrew

nut with setscrew

½" × 2½" machine bolt

⅛" × 3½" dia. steel plate

screw with nut to project 4" into handle

Illus. 20—Bench press.

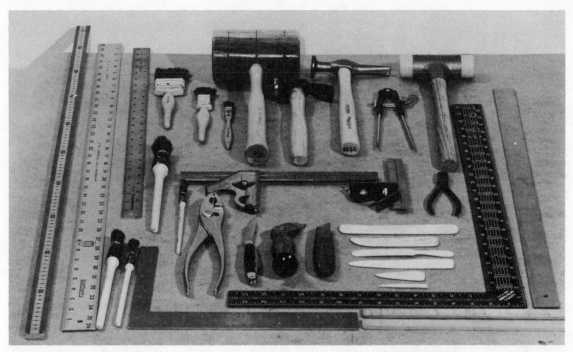

Illus. 21—Some useful tools: (left) metre stick, aluminum yard stick, 2-ft. rule, brushes for glue and paste, 9″ × 12″ steel square, 16″ × 24″ carpenter's framing square; (right) maple rubbing sticks (foreground), steel straightedge; various bone folders, Stanley Utility knife, mat-cutting knife, pocket knife, pliers, adjustable square with 12″ rule, same with 6″ rule, diagonal wire cutters, dividers; (top, right to left) plastic-faced mallet, rounding hammer, backing hammer, wooden mallet.

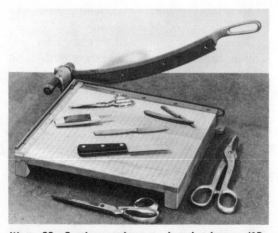

Illus. 22—Cutting equipment: board trimmer (15-, 24-, or 30-inch size), small scissors, large scissors, 12-inch tinsnips for rough-cutting boards, mat-cutting knife, straight razor (or single-edged razor blades), stainless steel table knife and butcher knife (blades broken off, ground and sharpened).

Illus. 23—Some ideas for weights, used in glueing, pressing, etc. chunks of metal, marbles, etc., cast in plastic; $7\frac{1}{2}$-lb. fire bricks, fitted with handles screwed to wood crosspieces glued on with epoxy glue; concrete pyramidal block, cased in tempered hardboard, stuck on with contact cement. Finish bricks with several coats of cellulose ester or brushing lacquer to prevent dusting.

15

Illus. 24—Some bookbinding adhesives: ground hide (or animal) glue, scales for weighing; polyvinyl acetate glue (or Elmer's Glue-All), liquid hide glue, a cake of bookbinders' flexible hide glue; non-warping paste.

ultimate amateur bindery press, this is indispensable for the school room. In this home-made version, the expensive handwheel has been replaced by inexpensive steel rods. Holes for the rods are bored through alternate faces of the hex nut and into the body of the 1½-inch screw. The ends of the rods are slotted with a hacksaw, steel wedges are positioned in the slots, and the rods are then driven into their respective holes. The rods are thus firmly wedged in place.

A large ball-bearing under the press screw reduces friction and permits great pressure to be applied. A car's front-wheel bearing large enough to accept the press screw makes a good thrust bearing.

SMALL TOOLS, KNIVES, ETC. (See Illus. 21–22–23).

ADHESIVES. (Illus. 24). Ground hide glue is the traditional book adhesive. Ground animal glue, which is similar, can also be used. Also, liquid hide glue. These glues are used in two forms: hard glue and flexible glue (see page 156 for preparation of dry ground and liquid glues). Polyvinyl acetate glue (white

glue) is also satisfactory for use on the back of a book, as it dries flexible. It is available practically everywhere in the U.S. under the trade-name Elmer's Glue-All.

Such items as bookbinders' cake flexible glue, and some foreign-made resin glues for single-sheet binding are available from professional bookbinding supply houses.

Dried ground glue must be heated for use. This is the best glue for covering with book cloth, paper, etc. It can be prepared in a coffee can or similar container, which is then placed in a larger pan containing water, after the manner of a double boiler. The glue is kept hot on an electric grill with the heat turned low. A candy or cooking thermometer will help you keep the temperature between 125–150° F. (51–65° C.) Too much heat destroys the strength of the glue; so also does frequent reheating, so, unless you contemplate large-scale production, prepare glue in small quantities.

Better than the above arrangement is an automatic electric fondue pot (Illus. 83). Keep the rheostat at LOW and do not let the water run dry. If the bottom of the fondue pot is oddly shaped, a piece of heavy-gauge, $\frac{1}{2}$-inch wire mesh will support the glue can.

Also available at somewhat more expense is the electric glue pot (Illus. 214), which requires no water. An extra glue container should be purchased with it—one for hard glue, the other for flexible glue.

PASTE. Non-warping mounting pastes, made without water, are available commercially. They are supplied to the bookbinding and picture-framing trades. Just as good, however, is ordinary flour paste made according to the formula given on page 157. Water-based paste warps, however, and special treatment is needed when it is used. This will be discussed more fully when the need arises.

Library paste, purchased from a stationer, can be used for some pasting operations, such

Illus. 25—Books and magazines suitable for hand binding.

as pasting up sections, pasting endpapers together, and so on.

Mending paste for book repair is used for repairing torn pages. A formula for making your own is given on page 157.

2. Materials Used in Bookbinding

Sewing Materials

SEWING THREAD. No. 20, 2- or 3-cord, unbleached linen thread, waxed, is standard for general sewing. Unwaxed thread should be drawn over a cake of beeswax before using it to sew with. No. 16 linen thread, heavier than No. 20, is suitable for large books with thick, soft sections. For very thin paper sections, or as a substitute for linen thread, use cotton-covered polyester thread. Polyester is a very strong synthetic fibre. Spooled for sewing machine use, it comes in one size only and is stronger when used doubled. Polyester 4-cord crochet thread is also a good thread for sewing thick, soft-paper sections. It is heavier than No. 20 and must be drawn over a cake of beeswax before use to wax it. Another use for this thread is discussed in Chapter 13, in connection with "perfect" binding, a method of binding books of single sheets without sewing.

Avoid white (bleached) linen carpet and button thread, as well as similar thread of cotton. The bleached thread rots and completely loses its strength in far less than 20 years, though the black thread and possibly some of the colored ones appear to hold their strength, but color makes them unsuitable for sewing books.

NEEDLES. Bookbinding needles have oval eyes and blunt points. A darning needle will serve if you first blunt the point on a whetstone. This will prevent pricking your fingers when you reach inside a section to receive the needle. Also keep a sharp-pointed, large needle on hand for perforating sections and endpapers in certain styles of sewing. If the needle is gripped in a pin-vice, it will be easier to handle.

TAPE. Bookbinding tape is a cotton twill tape, $\frac{1}{2}$ inch wide. Ordinary twill tape available at a sewing supplies counter is also suitable.

SEWING CORD. A soft, linen twine is the best sewing cord. Also suitable is hemp package twine or similar. The cord must be strong, durable, and flexible, and you must be able to fray the ends out into a thin wisp of material. Use 3-, 4-, or 6-ply, depending on the size and weight of the book.

Backing Materials

SUPER. A loosely woven, stiffly starched crash. A substitute is tarlatan, crinoline, or cheesecloth heavily starched.

BACKING CLOTH. Unbleached muslin. Starch it lightly before use to render it stiff enough and iron flat. Used on large, heavy books.

BACKING PAPER. Kraft (brown) paper, about the weight of that in a grocery carry-home bag. Or, an inexpensive, medium-weight, white drawing paper (cartridge paper in England); or single-ply, kid finish Bristol board (called "card" in Commonwealth countries).

NEWSPAPER. Old newspapers find a multitude of uses in the bindery. Cut them into single sheets and each sheet in half. Use them to protect the table top as well as the book when pasting or glueing. Newspaper is also used for lining the boards when pasting cover material with water-base paste.

BOARDS. These constitute the "hard covers" that make a book cost so much more than the paperback edition. Binder's board (or binder board) is best if you can get it—it is called "mill board" in Britain. Many art supply stores stock "chipboard" (a form of cardboard, not to be confused with the wood panel product) and "pulp board." Paper houses also handle these materials, but often a minimum purchase is required that is quite unreasonable for the amateur.

When rebinding old books, the original boards can often be used again, after being trimmed down to the new size of the book.

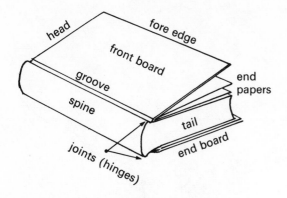

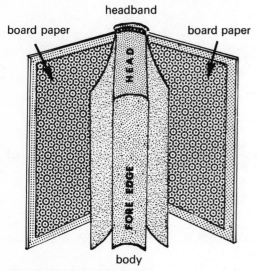

Illus. 26—Book nomenclature.

Also, save all bits of solid cardboard that come your way—shirt boards, stuffers from stocking and candy boxes, tablet backs, and so on. You can even make boards by pasting or glueing layer upon layer of paper together and letting it dry under a weight. Make sure the grain runs the same way in all the pieces.

Ordinarily, a board about $\frac{3}{32}$ inch thick is suitable for most books. The board can be thinner for a small book, thicker for a large one. Judgment and intuition play a part in selecting board of the right thickness.

ENDPAPER. Endpapers protect the body of the book from the strain of opening the boards. They constitute a kind of buffer. Often, especially in publishers' bindings, the end-

papers are made from the same stock as the book is printed on. Your chance of locating such a paper is practically nil. If you can find a paper house that will sell a small quantity, buy a medium-weight (about 70 lb.) book paper of medium grade, white wove finish. Otherwise, use a light- or medium-weight drawing paper. Colored papers such as construction paper, pastel paper, charcoal drawing paper, and so on, can be used for the board paper and the first fly leaf. You can also print your own designs on endpaper stock—first cut the design in linoleum, then print it, using the screw press as detailed in Chapter 14.

Another way to get colored paper is to take your regular white endpaper stock and soak it in a small quantity of water containing acrylic tube (artists') paint dissolved in it. Hang the paper up to dry. It will buckle, but soak it again in plain water (acrylic colors are waterproof), drain, and place between blotters to dry. Frequent changing of blotters will allow the paper to dry faster.

NOMENCLATURE OF THE BOOK. (Illus. 26). Each part of a book has a name of its own. The terminology shown in the illustration will be used throughout this book.

GRAIN. (Illus. 27). When paper, cardboard, etc., issue from the machine in the process of manufacture, the individual fibres of which the material is composed tend to orient themselves in a single direction, which is the direction in which the paper sheet is moving. This direction of fibre-orientation is called "with the grain." Crosswise to this direction is referred to as "across the grain."

There are several ways in which to determine the grain of paper, and this is important, as every piece of paper or cardboard that goes into a book must have its grain running in the direction of the height of the book. If you will fold a piece of paper with the grain, and another across the grain, and wet both folds, you will see why. When "with the grain" dries, it resumes its normal shape. But, when the crossgrain fold dries, it buckles. If this takes place at the back of a book, it can completely destroy your binding, as the back is constantly being wetted with paste and glue in the process.

Sometimes, as in kraft paper and cardboard, you can look at the surface of the material and actually see in which direction the grain runs. In paper taken from a roll, the grain runs with the roll, that is, it is wrapped round and round it. Some white papers with coarse grain need only to be held up to the light for the grain to become visible. Usually, cardboard and paper sold in large sheets have the grain running the long way of the sheet. This is not always true, so other means are used to check it out.

Take the two long edges of a cardboard sheet in your hands and attempt to bend it. If you feel little resistance, the grain runs parallel to your forearms. If you feel great resistance, the grain runs crosswise to your forearms.

To test a sheet of paper, roll it over on its long axis, so that the two edges are brought together. If there is little resistance and the paper collapses on itself, the paper is rolled with the grain. If there is much resistance, with the paper often snapping back instead of collapsing, it is rolled across the grain (see Illus. 27).

Another way to test paper for grain is to tear a strip along one edge. If the paper tears smoothly and evenly, you are tearing with the grain. If the tear runs irregularly and unpredictably at an angle, you are tearing across the grain.

Cover Materials

BOOKCLOTH. This is a lightweight, cloth material, made especially for bookbinding and available from binderies, binders' supply houses, etc. (See list of suppliers in Appendix.) It is impervious to moisture and is applied to the book with *hot glue*. It is available in many colors and textures.

BUCKRAM. A heavy, linen cloth, buckram is most often seen on public library books. Like bookcloth, it is purchased at the same places and is available in numerous colors. It is applied to the book with either non-warping or water-base paste. Buckram is very strong

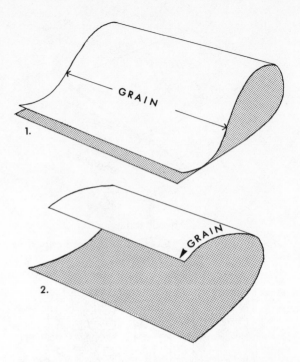

Illus. 27—(1) Paper rolled with the grain; (2) against the grain.

and durable and will far outlast other cover materials.

PLASTIC UPHOLSTERY MATERIAL. Available at department stores, mail-order houses, auto supply stores. Use only the cloth-backed; unbacked vinyl will not respond to ordinary glues and adhesives. Many such materials are printed with colorful patterns and are given an interesting texture. Some look and feel like leather. Plastic comes in numerous colors—choose only the type with the thin cloth backing—not the thick material.

CANVAS AND UNPREPARED CLOTH. Any kind of canvas or cloth—even silk—can be used to cover a book. Loose-leaf notebooks, ledgers and the like are often bound with a plain linen or cotton canvas cover. Hair canvas (it contains 18 per cent goat hair) makes a beautiful cloth covering.

These materials are not proof against penetration by moisture, hence glue must never be applied directly to the cloth. Polyvinyl acetate glue (Elmer's Glue-All) is particularly suitable as it turns clear when it dries and is therefore non-staining. The glue is brushed on the outer surface of the boards and on the hollow back (see page 67) and the book is let stand on the fore edge of its boards until the glue becomes tacky enough not to penetrate the cloth. Drape the cloth over the back and down the sides, patting it into contact. Instead of rubbing, use a photographers' print roller and roll the surface lightly to make the cloth adhere. Next, open the boards, apply Elmer's Glue-All to the inside margin. When tacky, turn in the cloth and roll it down. These manoeuvres are described in detail, using other covering materials, in chapters to come.

LEATHER. The leather used in bookbinding must be made especially for that purpose. Other kinds of leather are tanned in a different manner and are not as long-lasting. Leather is discussed more fully in the chapter devoted to leather bindings.

3. Book Structure and Preparation for Binding

The kind of book we are concerned with at present is one composed of folded sections, or signatures. A section can be determined by sight if you look at the back edge of the head of a book; there you can see that the folded sections are readily distinguished from each other.

In printing, a number of pages are printed on a large sheet of paper (see Book Sizes in Appendix), which is then folded as many times as required to make the section. You may have bought a book with uncut edges and had to cut through folds at the edges in order to be able to open up the pages. It is these folds that are trimmed off in most cases, forming the familiar, smooth cut edge of the book.

Ordinarily, a section contains 32 pages (16 leaves). So, if you start at the beginning of the book and count off 8 leaves, you should find the book opens to the middle of the section, where the sewing thread is visible. However, there sometimes may be more or fewer leaves to count, and this will have to be determined before you bind the book under consideration.

Magazine binding presents problems, some-times simple, sometimes difficult. A magazine which is stapled through the spine is called a "saddle-stitched" magazine. If a magazine is thin enough, a year's issue may be bound together, treating each magazine as if it were a section of a book.

Sometimes magazines consist either of folded sections or single sheets, with cover glued on, and pages secured with staples through the thickness of the publication. These are "side-stitched" magazines.

TEARING DOWN. Taking a book or magazine apart in order to rebind it is called "tearing down." In the matter of magazines or paper-bound books, the first step in tearing down is to remove the covers. Fold back the cover into the same plane as the body of the book and carefully tear it off by pulling it away from the back (Illus. 28).

Where staples exist, remove these by first lifting their bent-over ends with a staple-puller or a screwdriver and nipping them off (Illus. 29). Then turn the magazine over, lift the staple bows so that they can be gripped with pliers, and pull them out (Illus. 30).

Illus. 28—The first step in binding quality magazines is to tear off the front and back covers.

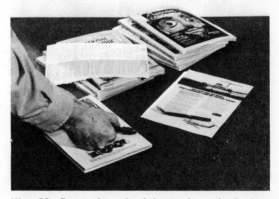

Illus. 29—Pry up the ends of the staples and snip them off with diagonal or end nippers.

Illus. 30—Lift the bow of the staples with a staple puller and pull out staples with pliers.

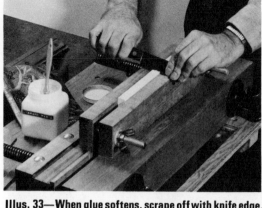

Illus. 33—When glue softens, scrape off with knife edge, drawing blade toward you. If necessary, repaste and scrape again.

Illus. 31—If you plan to bind in the cover of the magazine, trim off back edge smooth and straight.

Illus. 34—Open book to middle of first section, and cut the sewing thread stitches (bracketed arrows indicate location of stitches).

Illus. 32—The first step in rebinding a sewed-section paperback book is to remove the cover (see cover behind paste jar). Clamp the book in the lying press and apply paste thickly to back.

Illus. 35—Locate end of first section and carefully remove it from the body of the book. Continue through the book, cutting stitches and removing sections one at a time.

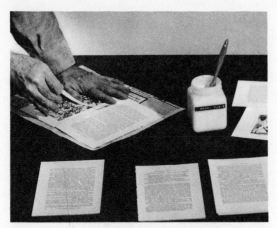

Illus. 36—Use a strip of thin, tough paper to repair the torn fold of the outside sheet of the section.

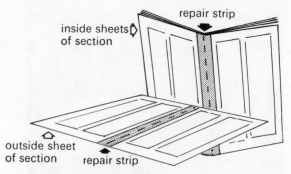

Illus. 37—Repairing torn folds of a section.

Guard strip is pasted to back side of cover and to end of section.

inside sheets of section

outside sheet of section

repair strip

repair strip

first section or signature of magazine

Illus. 38—Guarding in a magazine cover or loose illustration.

Whether it is a matter of binding a magazine cover in with the magazines, or a "floating" illustration in a book, the procedure is the same. First trim off the back edge smooth and even (Illus. 31).

THE PAPERBACK SEWED BOOK. First tear off the covers as described above and discard them —they are too stiff to bind into the book.

Place the book spine down in the glueing clamp (Illus. 40), and tighten the screws. Then pass the fore edge of the book between the bars of the lying press, supporting the clamp above the cheeks of the press with a couple of pieces of wood about $\frac{1}{4}$ inch thick. Tighten the lying press screws, remove the sticks from under the glueing clamp, loosen its screws and let it drop down on the large press, then retighten. The back now projects a quarter of an inch so that you can work on it. (Illus. 32).

Brush a thick coating of library paste on the back of the book and let sit about 5 minutes until the glue softens. When soft, scrape the glue and paste off with a knife blade (Illus. 33). It may be necessary to repeat this procedure a time or two, until all the old glue has been removed.

Open the book to the middle of the first section and cut the stitches of sewing thread (Illus. 34); then find the end of the section, open the book wide at that point and carefully

pull the section away in the same plane as the book (Illus. 35). Pick or scrape off any residue of glue still clinging to the fold. Do the same section by section until the book has been entirely torn down.

REPAIRING SECTIONS. In the process of tearing down, some of the sections are bound to be damaged; i.e., torn along the fold. Spread the sections out on the table and pick out those with a damaged outer sheet. Sometimes an inner sheet or two may also be damaged, but this is rare.

Choose a thin, bond paper for making repairs, or a rag content tracing paper, about 9 to 13 lb. weight. Such a repair is called a "guard strip," and too many, or too thick a paper will inordinately increase the swell at the back of the book.

Cut as many strips, $\frac{1}{2}$ inch wide, as there are

24

Illus. 39—Turn sections back edge to fore edge and place between plain pressing boards. Clamp in press overnight.

Illus. 40—After reassembling in correct order (collating) after pressing, jog the sections even at the head, then place in sawing clamp, jog even at the folds, and tighten the clamp screws.

sheets to be repaired. Use either a board trimmer or a straightedge and a sharp knife. Make sure that the grain of the paper runs the lengthwise direction of the strips.

Where the sheet to be repaired is an outer one, lay it outer face down on a sheet of newspaper, paste a guard strip with library paste and carefully rub it down along the torn fold on the *inside* of the sheet (Illus. 36). If the sheet is an inside one, adopt the opposite procedure. That is, paste down the guard strip along the *outside* of the fold (Illus. 37).

When all repairs have been made, any magazine covers or illustrations to be included have to be guarded in at their proper place as indicated in the drawing, Illus. 38.

Leave the pasted sheets spread out until dry, then carefully refold them and reassemble the sections. Stack the sections fore edge to back edge, alternating section by section; then place them between plain pressing boards and insert in the press under heavy pressure until the next day. This will drive out the air and press the freshly pasted work flat.

SAWING THE BACK. Upon removing the sections from the press, turn them around right way to, with all the folds on the same side. Go through and check each section for numerical order of the pages to be sure you have not

got one out of place or upside down. You must be eternally vigilant in this regard, because such things can and do happen, and regardless of how lovely your cover is, the book is spoiled.

Jog the book at the head (that is, hold the sections loosely in both hands and tap the head end of the book against the table) until the sections even up. Sections at the tail which are uneven are of no concern, as unevenness there is corrected in trimming.

Place the sections with folds down in the glueing clamp (Illus. 40) and jog the folds

Illus. 41—Marking the back for sawing.

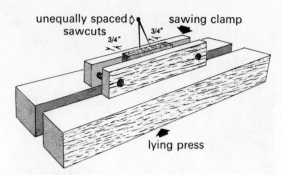

Illus. 42—Details of marking the back.

even. Then tighten the clamp. The back must be absolutely flat across and the head must be perpendicular to both sides of the book. If the sections have slipped out of square in handling, start over.

Again place the fore edge in the lying press and drop the glueing clamp. You are now ready to mark the back for sawing (Illus. 41–42).

The type of sewing we are about to undertake, the lock-stitch, requires that a sawcut be made across the back at each stitch.

Measure in ¾ inch from head and tail for the kettle-stitch sawcuts, then divide the space between into three or four *unequal* spaces

(Illus. 42). Mark the divisions across with a square and a felt-tip marker (Illus. 41). The spaces are purposely unequal so that it will be impossible for you to accidentally sew a section in upside down. Make all sawcuts just deep enough to pass through the innermost sheet of each section (Illus. 43). A dull saw will saw better than a sharp one, as the teeth will not catch.

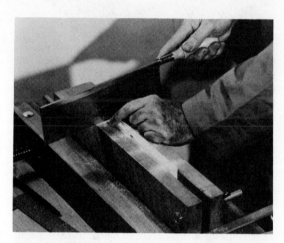

Illus. 43—With a fine-tooth saw, carefully saw the back across at each mark, just deep enough to penetrate the innermost fold of each section.

4. Sewing the Lock-Stitch

The lock-stitch is the simplest method of sewing, requiring no special equipment other than needle and thread. Although not as strong as the tape-sewn or cord-sewn book, it does not have either the bulk of tapes or the nuisance of cords where a thin book of few sections is involved.

THREAD. Use unbleached linen thread, #20 2-cord or 3-cord. For large, heavy books, #16 thread is generally used, but #20 thread, doubled, can be substituted for it. Linen book thread is sold in the form of half-pound cones. As a substitute, you may use cotton-covered polyester thread, white, if you double it.

SEWING. Seat yourself at a table, book face up in front of you, back edge about a foot from the edge, fore edge toward you, head of the book to your right. Turn over the first section, fold toward you, and lay it face down on the table (Illus. 45).

Snip off about 30 inches of thread and run it over a cake of beeswax and thread it into a blunt needle. Open the section to its middle and place a stick or ruler there to hold the place.

Pass the point of the needle into the section through the first sawcut at the head (kettle-stitch sawcut) and out through the last sawcut at the tail. (See Illus. 44A, 45).

Take a #11 crochet hook, reach into the section through one of the sawcuts and pull out a loop of the sewing thread. Do the same at each sawcut (other than the kettle-stitch cuts) (Illus. 46).

Continue sewing as indicated in the photos and captions (Illus. 44B, 47, and 48).

Remember to pull the slack out of the thread as you sew from stitch to stitch, and always pull the thread parallel to the back of the book. If you pull it out at right angles to the fold, you will tear the fold.

After sewing the second section, tie it to its own end with an ordinary granny or square knot, thus tying the two sections together. Thereafter, you will make use of the kettle-stitch (from the German word *Ketelstich*, meaning "chain stitch"). This stitch can be made in one movement as shown in Illus. 49; or, you can pass the needle behind the stitch below and pull it up until the thread forms a loop. Then pass the needle upward through the loop and pull the loop up firmly but do not make it too tight. Never pull the thread too tightly in making a stitch or tie, as it may cut through the section, or at least, result in less flexibility of the back.

To tie a new length of thread to the old, form a half loop or bend in the thread sticking

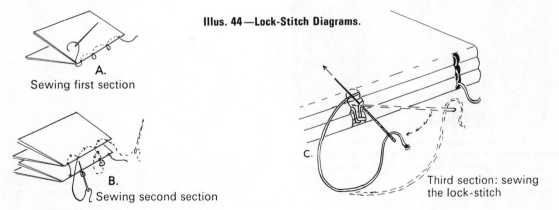

Illus. 44 —Lock-Stitch Diagrams.

A.
Sewing first section

B.
Sewing second section

C.
Third section: sewing the lock-stitch

Illus. 45—Pass the needle into the section at the right (head) and out at the tail. (See Illus. 44A.)

Illus. 46—Step two in sewing the first section: reach in through the middle sawcuts with a #11 crochet needle and pull loops of thread out through the sawcuts.

Illus. 47—Sewing on the second section. (Also see Illus. 44B.) Pass the needle in through the kettle-stitch saw cut at the tail and out at the next sawcut. Pass the needle upward through the loop of thread and back into the same saw cut and out at the next, and so on. At the head kettle-stitch sawcut, tie the thread to its own end.

Illus. 48—Sewing on the third section. (See Illus. 44C.) Pass the needle in through the head kettle-stitch sawcut and out through the first sawcut. Then upward behind the previous stitch and back into the third section. Repeat the stitch at each sawcut, then out through the kettle-stitch sawcut at the tail.

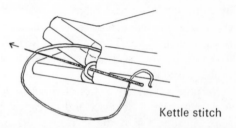

Kettle stitch

Illus. 49—The kettle-stitch. Pass the needle behind the previous stitch and through the loop formed by the thread. Pull snug.

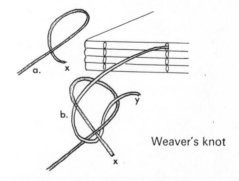

Weaver's knot

Illus. 50—The weaver's knot is used to tie a new length of thread to the old. By pulling on the ends x and y with the knot loose, the knot can be positioned so as to remain inside the section, between two stitches.

Illus. 51—Knocking down the swell. After first clamping in the sawing clamp, grip the fore edge of the book in the lying press and remove the clamp. Hold the knocking-down block against the book with one hand and strike along the back with a mallet.

out of the book (Illus. 50, y). Pass the new thread, x, through and around the half-loop as shown, then grasp the two ends, x and y, and manoeuvre the knot into a position that will cause it to lie *inside* the section as sewing continues. Then pull the knot tight and continue sewing.

When the last section is sewed, finish off the sewing by making two or three kettle-stitches, one under the other, then cut off the projecting ends of thread at start and finish of sewing about an inch long. These ends will be glued down to the back of the book.

KNOCKING DOWN THE SWELL. (Illus. 51). The extra thickness of thread at the back of the book adds to the thickness of the back. This is called "swell." It is removed, at least partially, by knocking down. As shown in the photo, hammer along folds with a wooden mallet, striking rather hard with the face of the mallet flat against the book. The edges of the mallet should be turned or rounded so as not to cut. After hammering one side, place the block on that side and hammer the other side. In most cases, the book paper is thick enough to allow

the thread to become embedded in it, thus reducing the amount of swell.

PASTING UP THE SECTIONS. (Illus. 52). Throw back the first two sections of the book. Lay newspaper on the first page of the third section, leaving a strip ⅛ inch wide exposed at the fold. Brush paste along this strip and close the second section on it. Treat the second section the same and close the first section on it. Turn the book over and paste up the last two sections the same way.

ENDPAPERS. Have endpapers made and ready. These consist of a single sheet of paper,

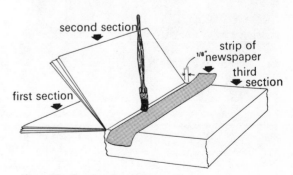

Illus. 52—Pasting down the sections.

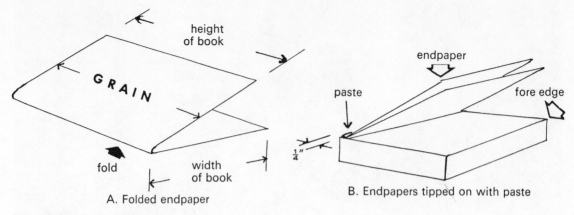

A. Folded endpaper

B. Endpapers tipped on with paste

Illus. 53—Tipped-on endpapers.

folded and trimmed to the size of the book (Illus. 53, 54). Brush paste on a strip $\frac{1}{4}$ inch wide at the back edge of the first section (Illus. 55), then position the endpaper and rub it down along the pasted strip (Illus. 56, 53B). This operation is called "tipping on" endpapers. Tipped-on endpapers are not the strongest construction, but they are the easiest to apply and require the least amount of material, hence are cheaper. All publishers' bindings use this type of endpaper.

When you have tipped on both endpapers, place a sheet of waxed paper on each side of the book and sandwich it between plain pressing boards. Place a brick or other heavy weight on top to keep the pasted sections from buckling and leave until the paste dries (a half hour or so) (Illus. 57).

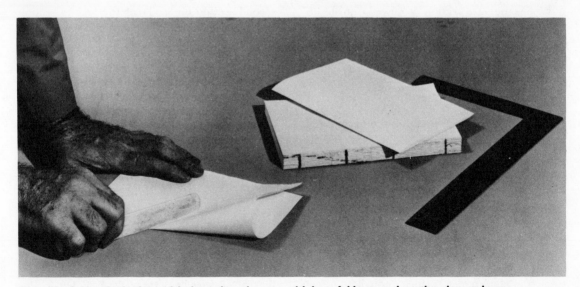

Illus. 54—Fold a single sheet with the grain and crease with bone folder to make a tipped-on endpaper.

Illus. 55—Brush paste along strip $\frac{1}{4}$ inch wide at back edge of book for attaching endpaper.

Illus. 56—Place endpaper on book and rub down along pasted strip at back edge of book.

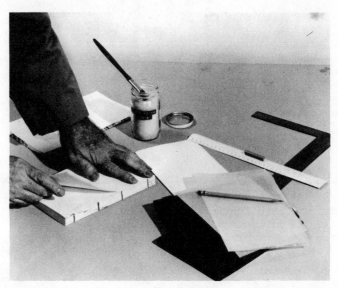

Illus. 57—Place waxed paper on both sides of book and sandwich between plain pressing boards. Leave under weight until paste dries.

Illus. 58—Brush flexible glue (or Elmer's Glue-All) over the back of the book. Rub in between the folds. A piece of waxed paper on each side of book keeps glue off clamp.

5. Trimming the Book

Trimming removes frayed, soiled edges from the book, at the same time reducing its size. Some publishers' editions have only the head trimmed, the fore edge and tail being left rough and uneven. In rebinding such a book, if not too soiled, the uneven edges can be left as they are and the head re-trimmed. The head is the edge that gathers most dust and thus gets dirtiest.

GLUEING UP THE BACK. (Illus. 58). See page 156 for how to make regular liquid hide glue flexible. Elmer's Glue-All might also be used, as polyvinyl acetate glues dry flexible. Let the book remain in the clamp until the glue becomes tacky—that is, still sticky but not sticky enough to adhere to a finger when touched.

Since the back of a book must be flexible so as to bend when the book is opened, never use a hard glue on the back.

Best is hot flexible glue, made thin enough to run readily off the brush and heated to its maximum temperature (150° F. or 66° C.).

PREPARATIONS FOR TRIMMING THE HEAD. Hone the point of the plow blade to a keen edge with a *hard* Arkansas stone (Illus. 59). If the blade has been seriously dulled, sharpen it first with a Washita or soft Arkansas stone, then finish with the hard stone. Remove the burr from the underside of the blade by drawing it flat across the face of the stone, edge trailing. Use plenty of oil on the stone(s), but be sure to wipe the blade entirely clean before using it.

The usual way to trim a book (under unexceptional circumstances) is to trim first the head, then the tail, and lastly, the fore edge.

First mark the head trim-line (Illus. 60) $\frac{1}{8}$ inch from the edge on the board paper. Use a square to make sure it is at right angles to the back.

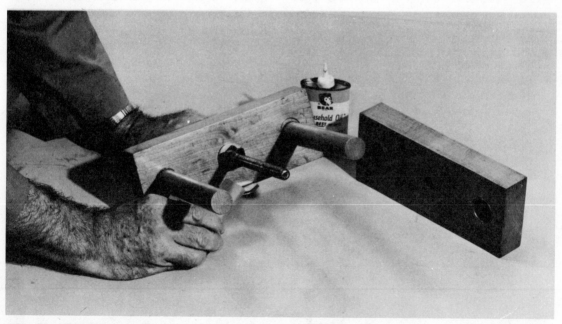

Illus. 59—While glue is setting, hone plow knife with a hard Arkansas whetstone. Don't take the plow apart as shown in photo. It was done here only to clarify the picture.

Illus. 60—Using a square, mark a trim-line across the head of the book, $\frac{1}{8}$ inch from the edge. This line must be perpendicular to the back of the book.

We are assuming here that the back of the book has little swell and is not appreciably thicker than the fore edge. If there is a slight extra thickness, this can be compensated for by laying sheets of paper step-fashion on the book as filler.

You will need a pair of "cutting boards," which can be either $\frac{1}{4}$-inch plywood or tempered hardboard large enough to cover the book with an inch or so over. Place a piece of

thin cardboard between the back cutting board and the book. This receives the point when the book is cut through, protects the cutting board and prevents undue wear of the cutting point.

Place the front cutting board on the book with its top edge along the trim-line marked on the board paper. Grip the board-and-book sandwich tightly to prevent slipping and insert it between the bars of the press from above. Take it with your other hand from below (Illus. 61) and work it downward until the front cutting board is even with the cheek of the front bar of the press. Turn up the press screws by hand until they grip the book.

Now check the book all around for straightness. Look down on it from above to make sure the back is straight across. Check it horizontally, looking between the press bars, to make sure the head is flat across and not running up- or downhill. When you are assured that the book is in straight, tighten the press, using the wooden handle that comes with the press screws

Illus. 61—Hold the book from below when adjusting it in the press for trimming the head.

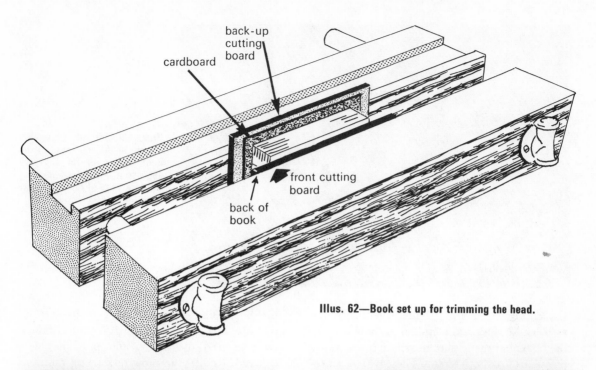

cardboard

back-up
cutting
board

front cutting
board

back of
book

Illus. 62—Book set up for trimming the head.

Illus. 63—Press down firmly on the plow while cutting to keep the blade from riding up and cutting a crooked edge.

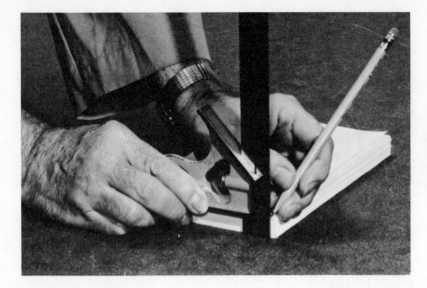

Illus. 64—Set the adjustable square to the thickness of the book and mark for the fore edge trim line $\frac{1}{8}$ inch in from the fore edge of the <u>narrowest</u> page.

(bench screws). Do not tighten them so much as to cause the press members to bow around the book, but *do* measure the space between the press bars over both screws. These two measurements must be equal for the press bars to be parallel to each other. When properly set up for trimming, the appearance will be as shown in Illus. 62.

TRIMMING THE HEAD. Place the plow on the press, *behind* the book, opened wide enough for the point to clear the book. Now turn the handle and run the point up to where it just touches the book. Pull the plow back to its starting position, hold it down firmly, give the handle a twist to feed the point, and pass the plow forward. Return the plow to starting position, again feed the point a little more and repeat the cutting stroke. (Illus. 63).

NOTE: When cutting the head or tail, feed the point to the book *only* on the *forward* stroke. If you try to cut toward the back, you may tear a chunk out of it.

Continue cutting a few pages at a time until the point is engaged by the backing cardboard.

Illus. 65—Mark the fore edge trim line at right angles to the trimmed head, using a square to ensure accuracy.

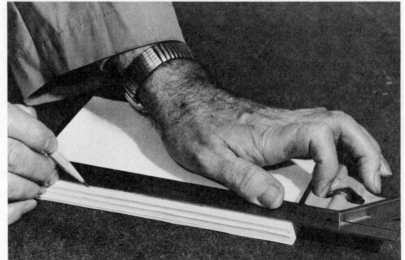

Illus. 66—A relatively inexpensive, office-type guillotine is fine for the advanced amateur. Note blade and how it trims fore edge of book. This machine will cut a book 1½ inches thick by 12 inches.

Illus. 67—Back view of the guillotine, showing the paper clamp and the adjustable guides that ensure accurate trimming.

Remove the book from the press, turn it over and repeat all the previous steps in preparation for and the actual trimming of the tail.

TRIMMING THE FORE EDGE. (Illus. 64). First mark for the fore edge line of trim, then draw the trim-line (Illus. 65). Insert the book in the press as before, with the fore edge up, and proceed to trim it with the plow. When trimming the fore edge, you can feed the point on both the forward and the back strokes and cut it twice as fast, since there is no fold to tear out.

THE GUILLOTINE. (Illus. 66–67). A professional-type paper cutter is called a "guillotine." This type is available in various capacities of cut and at varying prices. The advanced amateur bookbinder will find that the addition of a guillotine to his bindery will vastly speed up the task of trimming.

The use of the guillotine is not recommended for a classroom of young children, as a great deal of responsibility is involved in its use. The blade is large, heavy and very sharp.

In using the guillotine, the back-gauge (Illus. 67) is set for the dimension desired *after* trimming. The book is then placed on the platform, the edge to be trimmed under the blade, which is locked in place to prevent accident. With the handwheel at the front of the model shown (in some machines, it is on top), the clamp is brought down on the book and tightened. With one hand, the operator releases the blade lock and with the other brings down the handle. The blade cuts through a stack of paper without effort. The handle is then returned to its upright safety position, where the blade lock automatically engages. Loosen the clamp, reset the back gauge, and set the book under the clamp for the next trim. It can all be done more quickly than it takes to tell about it.

Such a guillotine is also a handy instrument for cutting stacks of paper into scratch pads. The blade can cut through the middle of a stack of paper of long dimension—something the press and plow arrangement is unable to do.

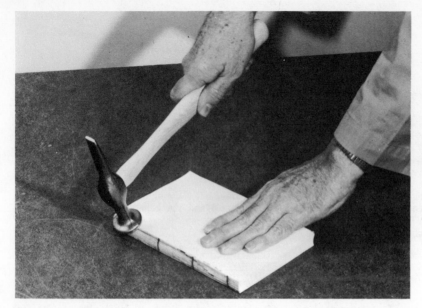

Illus. 68—Rounding the back of the book. This auto-body hammer is useful for this. The cross-peen is used to smooth and straighten tapes on a tape-sewn book. The backing hammer or wooden mallet can also be used. File the striking face to a bulge.

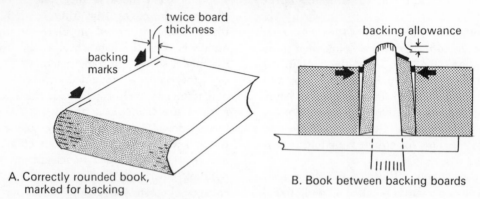

A. Correctly rounded book, marked for backing

B. Book between backing boards

Illus. 69—Preparing the book for backing.

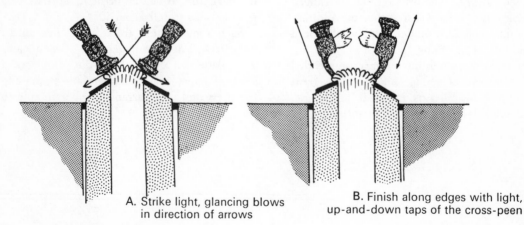

A. Strike light, glancing blows in direction of arrows

B. Finish along edges with light, up-and-down taps of the cross-peen

Illus. 70—Backing the book.

38

6. Rounding and Backing the Book

Rounding and backing are important operations, as the first gives the book its shape and the second assures that it keeps it.

Pick up a reasonably thick book and examine it. Note how the folds of the sections are bent each way from the middle. Observe the curved shape of the back and the fact that this curve is repeated by the inward curve of the fore edge of the book. Because of its shape, the book opens easily and stays open when opened out flat on a table.

ROUNDING. (Illus. 68, 69A). The book is rounded when the glue on the back has reached the tacky stage, when it is still soft enough to stretch in the formation of the round. If the book has been left too long and the glue has dried, wipe it with a wet cloth and wait 5 minutes or so for it to soften.

The full operation of rounding is not entirely visible in Illus. 68. Actually, the operator's thumb is pressed against the fore edge of the leaves so that, as the hammer is tapped lightly along the back edge, the thumb at the same time pushes the fore edge inward while the fingers, pressed tightly against the book, pull its upper surface toward the operator. Turn the book over and repeat the operation on the other side of the book. It will be necessary to turn the book back and forth several times before a nice round is achieved (Illus. 69A). Once the book has been shaped, leave it so until the glue dries. A pressing board and weight on top will hold it.

MARK FOR BACKING. Measure in at the head a distance equal to twice the thickness of the board (normally $\frac{3}{16}$ inch) and make a mark on

Illus. 71—The backing hammer in use. Movement of hammer is from left to right in a downward-sweeping curve.

Illus. 72—Clean old glue off back with paste and glue up with fresh, flexible glue. Center super backing cloth and rub down with fingers so that glue comes through.

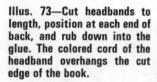

Illus. 73—Cut headbands to length, position at each end of back, and rub down into the glue. The colored cord of the headband overhangs the cut edge of the book.

the outside endpaper (board paper). Repeat the measurement at the tail, then turn the book over and mark the other side.

INSERT BOOK IN BACKING PRESS. Convert the lying press to a backing press by placing backing boards between the bars (Illus. 69B, 70, 71). The sloping edges of the boards are shod with steel, as they must withstand considerable punishment in the course of backing many books.

Insert the fore edge of the book between the backing boards, take it from below and care-fully adjust the book so that the backing marks line up with the edges of the backing boards. Tighten the press by hand enough to hold and examine the book to make sure it is straight in all directions and that the marks are lined up correctly.

Tighten the press with the screw handle, equally on both sides. The screws must be turned as tightly as possible without bowing the press bars. Measure the space between the bars at each screw and adjust until both spaces are equal.

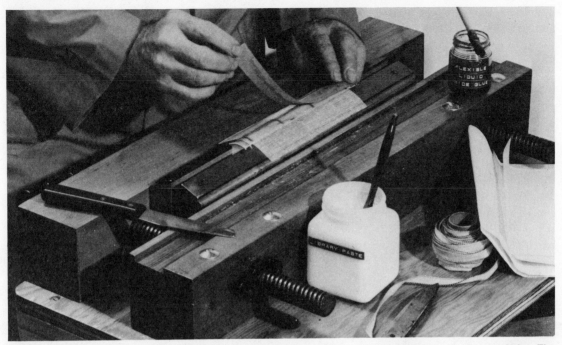

Illus. 74—Glue a strip of heavy kraft or drawing (cartridge) paper over the super, applying a fresh coat of glue. The paper is as wide as the curve over the back and long enough to cover both headbands.

Illus. 69B demonstrates how the pressure is applied at the edges of the cheeks of the press (arrows), so that the backing steels grip the book tightly, while the boards flare somewhat apart at the bottom and thus avoid marking a crease along each side.

BACKING. (Illus. 70, 71). The backing hammer shown is a professional type, used by bookbinders. A rawhide or wooden mallet may also be used, or a plastic-faced hammer. The important thing about the hammer or mallet is that the face must be rounded, even bulging, with no sharp edges.

Before actually striking the book, practice a few swing strokes in the air over it. Do not apply force; let the weight of the hammer do the work. Start at one end of the back and gently hammer along its length, causing the edge sections to begin to turn. You are not trying to hammer the fold completely over with one stroke. If you manage to bend it over 10 per cent of the way, that is enough. Return down the other side of the book, swinging the

hammer in the opposite direction. Keep up this forth-and-back swinging of the hammer until the outside sections are fully turned over against the steels and the inner folds are bent over less and less toward the middle of the book, where they are upright. Turn the hammer over and tap with the peen along both edges of the book to crease the outermost section; or use the rounded edge of a mallet. (Illus. 70B). Finally, take a bone folder and rub the back down all over, with special attention to the edges.

While the book is still between backing boards, brush paste on the back, wait a few minutes, and scrape off the paste and old glue. Reglue with fresh, hot glue or Elmer's Glue-All rubbed well in between the sections. Leave in press until the glue dries.

If a number of people are working, as in a classroom, and the backing press may not be tied up for long periods of time, the book may be removed immediately after backing, placed between plain pressing boards and gripped in

41

a bench press, where the back is then cleaned and re-glued.

BACKING CLOTH. (Illus. 72). The backing cloth serves two purposes: (1) it strengthens the back, (2) it provides hinges to which the boards are attached. For most purposes, a form of crash is used, called "super." As a substitute, tarlatan, crinoline, or cheesecloth that has first been stiffly starched, can be used.

With a flexible rule, measure the width of the back over the curve and the distance from head kettle stitches to tail kettle stitches. The super should be cut wide enough to overhang the back $1\frac{1}{4}$ inches on each side, and should reach from kettle stitch to kettle stitch (Illus. 73).

Rub the super down into the fresh glue.

HEADBANDING. (Illus. 73). Technically, the band at the head of the book is the headband, and the one at the tail is the tailband. Both are loosely referred to as headbands.

If you will examine a book from a boarded edition, you will usually find headbands covering the folds of the sections. They are not a necessity, but they do brighten up the appearance of a book. Headbanding material is inexpensive and available in various colors. It is sold in lots of a number of yards. The material is about an inch wide, made of cloth, with a bead along one edge displaying spots of alternating color. This bead overhangs the cut edge of the book.

On very fine bindings made by bookbinding craftsmen, the headbands are sewed on in the form of colored threads of silk. These not only provide strengthening of the cover when tipping a book backward off the shelf with a finger on top, but, being sewed into the sections themselves, cannot be torn loose. In Chapter 12, instructions are given for making headbands sewed with colored thread and glued to the back of the book.

PADDING THE BACK. (Illus. 74). In commercially bound books, padding is hardly ever applied over the super. However, padding adds strength to the back and prevents the cloth spine from sticking to the back of the book by accident.

The padding is composed of a strip of kraft or soft drawing (cartridge) paper cut to the width and length of the back. At the same time, cut a second piece the same size to form the "loose hollow" when the book is covered.

Brush hot, flexible glue over the entire back, including the headbands and lay the strip of backing paper in place. Rub it down with a bone folder (Illus. 75) until well adhered.

Leave the book in press until the glue has had a chance to set, preferably until the next day.

Illus. 75—Rub backing paper down with a bone folder until it is well adhered. Leave book in press until glue dries.

Illus. 76—The most accurate way to cut boards is with a steel straightedge and a sharp knife. Hone the blade on a soft Arkansas stone or an India stone.

7. Casing In

Many ways of covering a book have been developed and the simplest of these is called "casing in," the method generally used in book manufacture. The cover material and the boards are first assembled as a unit separate from the book, then are attached to it in the final glue-down of the board papers.

There are two ways to make a case—the "tight-joint" style and the "French-groove" style. The former style has no groove at the back edge of the boards and the latter does. Otherwise, the two styles receive the same treatment in casing in.

THE BOARDS. The boards form the so-called "hard cover," as distinguished from "paperback" in publishers' language. Binder's board (mill board in England) is the preferred material, but other cardboards may be used as already explained. For what you would think of as an "ordinary book," a board of the thickness (calibre) of about $\frac{3}{32}$ inch (exactly 0.09375 inch or 2.381 mm) is generally used. A board as thin as 0.082 inch (about 2.08 mm) is satisfactory for most books. If a heavier board (0.125 to 0.1040 inch $=\frac{1}{8}$ to $\frac{9}{64}$ inch $=$

3.175 to 3.572 mm) is available, it can be used for books larger than about 8vo (octavo) in size. However, a thin piece of pulpboard or cardboard can be pasted or glued to the heavier board to make up the desired thickness. This is often done when making "split boards" (see Chapter 8).

Of course, you do not need to rush out and buy a micrometer for measuring board thicknesses. You can tell by twisting the board a bit whether it is strong enough by itself or should be reinforced. If you have nothing but thin shirtboards (stiffeners in new shirt packing), you can glue or paste three or four thicknesses together.

Except for the thinnest cardboard, it is inadvisable to cut boards with a board trimmer, as the knife tends to crush the edge, making it impossible to achieve a square, accurate edge in covering. A steel straightedge and a mat knife will cut the edges square and accurately (Illus. 76). Where the board bulges up from the cutting pressure, flatten it by rubbing with the end of a folder (Illus. 77). Do not try to cut entirely through the board with one

sweep of the knife. First, draw the point *lightly* along the straightedge. This forms a "track" which guides subsequent knife strokes and prevents the blade from running askew. The knife should be whetted to a keen edge beforehand, on a *soft* Arkansas stone, or an India stone.

Another way to cut boards accurately is first to cut them out roughly to size with a pair of tin snips. Then stick them together with a couple of tiny spots of paste between them. Mark the head trimline as you would for a book and trim off the excess cardboard with press and plow. Cut all four edges before separating the boards.

MEASURING BOARDS FOR TIGHT JOINT. (Illus. 80A). The amount by which the board overhangs the book all around is called "the square." This is generally the same on all three sides, though sometimes you will see a book having the fore edge wider. The square amounts to $1\frac{1}{2}$ times the board thickness and this figure is added to the width of the book from the turn-up to the fore edge to get the width of the boards. Twice this figure is added to the height of the book to get the height of the boards. You can simplify this by making the square equal to $\frac{1}{8}$ inch all around, up to $\frac{3}{16}$ inch for large books.

Illus. 78—Trim the back corners of the board with a razor blade to form the nick. A piece of sheet aluminum protects both book and blade.

MEASURING BOARDS FOR FRENCH GROOVE. (Illus. 80B). The board width in this case is equal to the width of the book from the turn-up to the fore edge of the board paper. The height of the board is equal to the height of the book plus 3 times the board thickness (or $\frac{1}{4}$ inch, if preferred). When the board is moved away from the turn-up $1\frac{1}{2}$ times its own thickness (or $\frac{1}{8}$ inch), the fore edge square comes into being, an equal space being left at the back, forming a groove between the back edge of the board and the turn-up.

Keep it in mind that the grain in the boards must run vertically, the same as for paper used in the book.

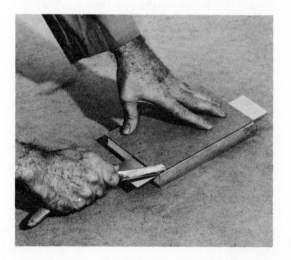

44

Illus. 79—Book at left has boards prepared for tight joint (note nicks at back corners). Book at right has boards prepared for a French groove—note space between back edge of board and turn-up of backing.

TRIMMING BACK CORNERS OF BOARDS. (Illus. 78, 80C). This is done only in the case of a tight joint. Its purpose is to increase the flexibility of the hinge at the corner and to prevent the rapid wear of the cover that would otherwise ensue. Cut the "nick" with a razor blade, after the board is positioned on the book. A piece of sheet aluminum or thin cardboard under the cut will protect the book.

MEASURING BOOK CLOTH FOR THE COVER. (Illus. 81, 82). With a framing square, mark a right angle on the back side of the cloth and another $\frac{3}{4}$ inch in to indicate the turn-in, where the cloth will be turned over the edges of the boards. The cover will be more flexible and durable along the hinges if the height of the book runs parallel to the selvedge of the book cloth. Trim the selvedge off when cutting out the cover material. If you can hold the boards in place by hand while turning the book as shown in Illus. 81, well and good. However, if they tend to slip, first stick the boards to the book with a couple of tiny dots of paste.

Place the book on the cloth as indicated in Illus. 81, then roll it over its spine (without slipping!), to lie on its other side. Mark the edge of the cloth $\frac{3}{4}$ inch from the fore edge of the book, and cut out the cover.

MAKING THE CASE. Illustrations 82 to 91 provide a step-by-step description of case-

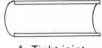

A. Tight joint.

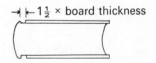

B. French groove.

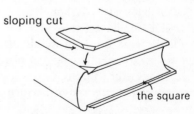

C. Trim off back corners of boards.

Illus. 80—Preparing the boards.

45

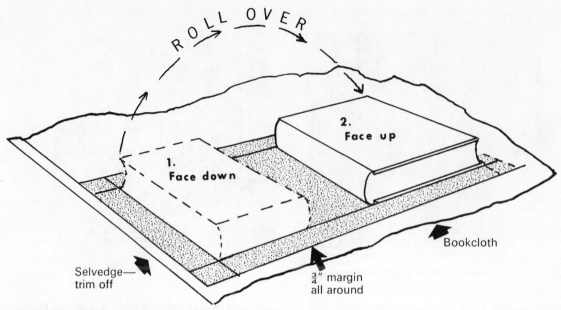

Illus. 81—Measuring length of cover material.

making, so it will not be repeated here. As soon as the cover material has been turned in over the edges of the boards, the case is placed on the book, the squares adjusted, and the book put to press. It is a good idea at this point to insert a piece of thin flashing aluminum (used by roofers and available at hardware stores) between each board and the body of the book. Place waxed paper between the boards and the metal sheets to keep the metal clean. The metal sheets provide a stiff plane for the squares to bear against, so that the freshly glued cover material is pressed flat against the underside of the board, where otherwise it might come unglued along the squares and bulge instead of being neatly square and flat.

GLUEING THE COVER. The best glue for covering with book cloth is hot, liquid, hide glue. The glue should be thin and runny—running off the glue brush in a thin stream. Such glue is slow to set, allowing you plenty of time to work the cover—that is, to rub it down and work it over the edges into the turn-in.

Illus. 82—In cutting book cover material, let the height of the book run parallel to the selvedge of the cloth. Use a square to mark cloth for cutting.

Liquid hide glue, a ready-prepared cold glue preparation, can also be used for covering. It is a little thick, but it brushes out well and is also slow drying enough to give you plenty of time in which to work over the cover.

Glue is used on book cloth, artificial leather, cloth-backed plastic upholstery material, and similar materials. It is also used on untreated canvas and cloth, procedures which will be explained later on in this book.

46

Illus. 83—Bookcloth responds best to thin, hot, __hard__ glue, heated in a double boiler. (Automatic electric fondue pot is shown with can of glue in a water bath.) Brush glue over entire inside surface of cloth. If corners tend to curl, weight them down.

Illus. 84—Covering the tight-joint book. Position book, with boards held in place, on the cloth as shown.

Keep the temperature of the glue in the pot at 150° F. (66° C.). The candy or cooking thermometer is marked SCALD MILK at this temperature, so it is easy to keep track of. Do not let the temperature of the glue drop below 125° F. (52° C.).

TRIMMING OUT THE CASE. When thoroughly dry, the case is removed from the book and the margins are trimmed. It is a good idea to mark one of the boards and the endpaper belonging to it, so as not to get the case turned around. If everything is exact, this would make no

Illus. 85—Place the hollow-back strip of kraft paper with one edge against the back of the book and rub it down on the glued cloth. This strip keeps the cover from becoming glued to the back of the book.

Illus. 86—Bring the far edge of the cover over the back and carefully (making sure it is straight) bring it into contact with the board. Pull the cloth tight against the back and rub it down on the board with a folder.

difference, but it seldom is, so it is well to work the case through to the end with the same board against the same side all the way.

Take a pair of dividers and make little punch marks $\frac{3}{8}$ inch from the edge. This is the final width of margin. Trim out all the excess cover material with knife and straightedge (Illus. 94). Take care to cut not quite up to the back edge

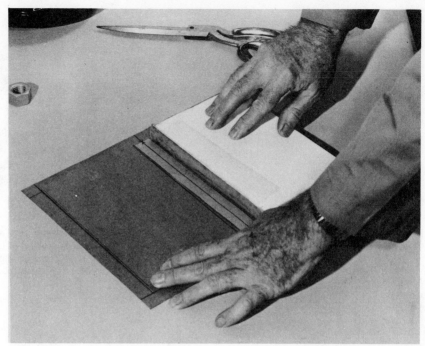

Illus. 87—Lay the cover back with the board adhered to it.

of the boards, or you will cut right through the case at the back and spoil it then and there. And you will have the whole job to do over.

GLUEING DOWN THE BOARD PAPERS. (Illus. 95–96). Fit the case again around the book and throw back the front cover. Place a sheet of newspaper under the board paper to protect the book. Using the same glue you used on the cover, brush glue under the tab of super, then brush the super down into the glue. Apply glue to the entire boardpaper, then carefully bring the board over and place its back edge squarely at the joint. Now lower the board onto the glued board paper, just enough to

Illus. 88—Lay the body of the book aside. The case is now ready for turning in the cover material.

Illus. 89—First, cut off all four corners of the cloth at a 45-degree angle, $\frac{1}{4}$ inch from the corners of the boards.

Illus. 90—Turn the cloth in at head and tail and rub it down to adhere it to the margins of the boards and across the hollow-back strip.

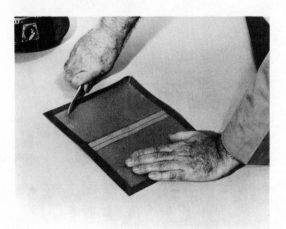

Illus. 92—Tie up the joint of the tight-joint book with string or sewing thread to pull the cloth down into the nicks cut at the back corners of the boards. Shape the cloth corners at head and tail with a pointed folder.

Illus. 93—Finally, slide the book back in between the pressing boards until their edges are even with the back edge. Apply pressure (with the wingnuts, in the case of this book press) and leave overnight.

stick. Lift and check to see if the boardpaper is on straight. If not, peel it off and try again. When straight, slip a piece of waxed paper under the newspaper, which you then discard, and press the cover down firmly on it. Open the board and rub the board paper down with

Illus. 91—Turn in the fore edges and rub them down.

50

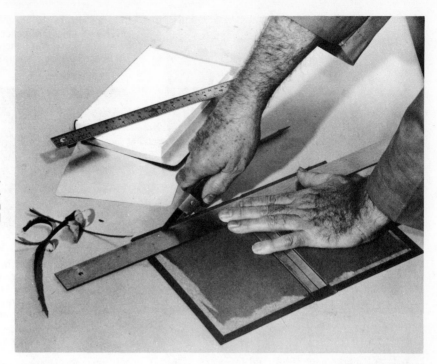

Illus. 94—Trim out the excess turn-in, leaving a margin $\frac{3}{8}$ inch wide. Do not trim across the back, or you will cut through the cloth.

your hand, then close the board again. Turn the book over and glue down the second board paper.

PRESSING. (Illus. 97). When pressing a book with a tight joint, use plain pressing boards, keeping their edges even with the back edges of the boards, as before. When pressing a book with a French groove, use grooving

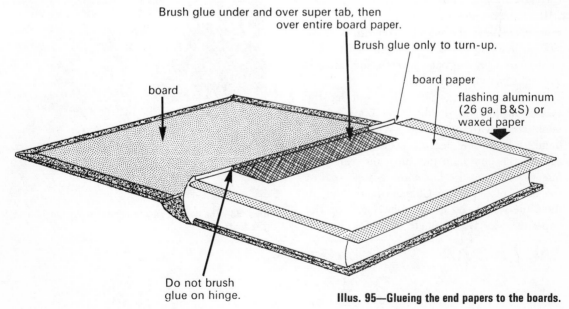

Brush glue under and over super tab, then over entire board paper.

Brush glue only to turn-up.

board

board paper

flashing aluminum (26 ga. B&S) or waxed paper

Do not brush glue on hinge.

Illus. 95—Glueing the end papers to the boards.

Illus. 96—Brush the same hot, hard glue used on the cover over the board paper. Newspaper protects book from glue. Note candy thermometer in glue can as an aid in maintaining temperature.

Illus. 97—Books pressing in the screw press. Note book with tight joint on bottom between plain pressing boards; book on top has French grooves shaped with grooving boards. Jaws are $\frac{1}{8}'' \times \frac{3}{4}''$ strip aluminum with edges planed down to $\frac{1}{16}''$ and rounded.

boards and make sure the metal jaws are *in the grooves* and not bearing against either of the boards. The latter is a very fast way to ruin your work.

OPENING THE BOOK. (Illus. 98). The book should remain in press at least until the next day; then you can remove it and open it correctly.

If a book is suddenly opened for the first time somewhere near the middle, you run a grave risk of breaking its back. The only cure for a book with a broken back is rebinding. Here is the right way to open a book:

Stand the book on its spine and let the boards drop open, holding the body of the book erect with one hand. With the other hand, take a few leaves, press them down against the board on that side and run your fingers with pressure down the gutter, against the body of the book. Change hands and, in the same way, press down a few pages on the opposite side. Go through the book in this manner, alternating from side to side and rubbing down the leaves, until you reach the middle. A book so opened has been properly treated and will remain flexible without danger of a broken back.

Illus. 98—The correct way to open a newly bound book (see text).

8. Sewing a Book on Tapes

The strongest sewing is done on tapes; therefore it is the ideal sewing for large, heavy books, though tape-sewing is not confined to such books. The method may be used with any book.

Professional bookbinding tape comes in a roll, is cotton twill and $\frac{1}{2}$ inch wide. However, the cotton twill tape you can buy at a sewing notions counter is also $\frac{1}{2}$ inch wide and is equally suitable for use. Sometimes, you may be able to find such sewing tape in brown, unbleached linen.

A maximum of 4 tapes will be enough for practically any book, though more can be added if necessary. The minimum number of tapes is two for books under 8vo (octavo) in size (see Book Sizes in Appendix). 8vo and larger require 3 to 4 tapes, depending on thickness and weight.

Tape-sewing is also ideal for binding single-fold, saddle-stitched magazines that are not too bulky, where each issue can serve as a section in the volume. Often-used reference books, school books, shop and laboratory manuals, and all books destined for hard service or abuse, are best sewed on tapes.

PREPARING THE BOOK FOR BINDING. For the demonstration, a two-volume set of section-sewed paperback has been chosen. The two books are first torn down, combined into one volume, and prepared for sewing as discussed in Chapter 3. A book bound in hard covers is torn down as demonstrated in Chapter 11.

MAKING "SEWED ENDPAPERS." Sewing endpapers into the book makes it stronger. The front endpaper is laid waste leaf down and sewed the same as if it were the first section or signature (Illus. 114). After sewing the last book section, lay on the final endpaper waste leaf up and sew it on, then secure the sewing with a couple of kettle stitches.

Illus. 99 diagrams the construction of "accordion pleat" sewed endpapers (called

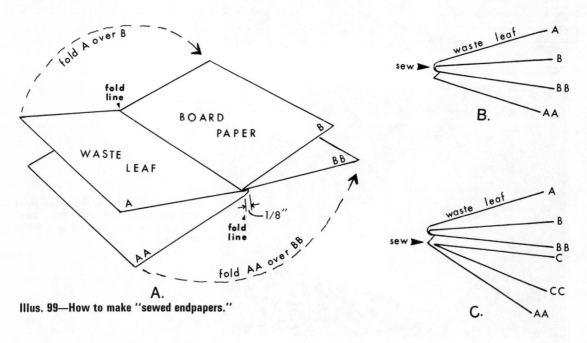

Illus. 99—How to make "sewed endpapers."

Illus. 100—Cut two pieces of paper (for each endpaper set), $\frac{1}{2}$ inch wider (with the grain) than the height of the book, and $\frac{1}{2}$ inch longer (across the grain) than twice its width. Fold each sheet down the middle, with the grain, and crease the fold with a folder.

Illus. 101—Place some newspaper over and under the folded sheet, leaving a strip $\frac{1}{8}$ inch wide along the fold exposed. Brush paste on the strip.

Illus. 102—Lay the second folded sheet over the first, fold over fold, overlapping $\frac{1}{8}$ inch. Rub down with folder to adhere.

Illus. 103 — Place the pasted sheets between waxed paper and under a pressing board and weight. Repeat foregoing operations with second set of papers. Leave under weight until dry— about $\frac{1}{2}$ hour.

"zigzag endpapers" by British binders). A century ago, commercial binders often constructed the endpapers as shown in Illus. 99B. Though this construction saved paper, it was not neat, as the sewing showed between the board paper and the first flyleaf when the board was opened out. For a neater job with invisible sewing; a second folded sheet (C-CC) is added (Illus. 99C), and the endpaper is sewed through the fold next to the book. The stitches then come between two flyleaves and are hidden in the turn-up made in backing the book.

Illus. 100–106 provide a step-by-step demonstration of making sewed endpapers. Two sets are to be made. Use a white, medium-grade book paper such as a white wove offset of 70-lb. (U.S.) weight. Such a paper is about 50 per cent heavier than standard, 20-lb. bond typing paper, having a caliper (thickness) of about 0.005″. This should be approximately equivalent to the paper composing the book, or even heavier, depending on whether the book paper is hard or soft.

MARKING THE BACK. Clamp the assembled

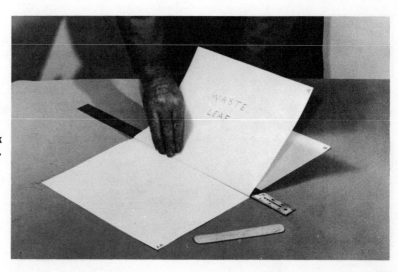

Illus. 104—Fold waste leaf A back over a metal ruler upon sheet B. (See diagram, Illus. 99.)

Illus. 105—The second fold forms the "accordion pleat," Folding sheet AA back over sheet BB.

sections, without endpapers, in the press and draw lines across the back, $\frac{3}{4}$ inch in from head and tail, to mark the location of the kettle stitches. Next, take a pair of dividers, set them to slightly wider than the width of the tapes, and mark random locations on the back for up to 4 tapes (Illus. 107). Then take a square and mark lines straight across the back with a fine-point, felt-tip marker (Illus. 108). Make sure that each and every fold is marked, for you will later have to locate these marks and puncture them with a needle, for only the kettle-stitch locations are sawed in the tape-sewn book (Illus. 109).

If the book is a heavy one, it is a good idea to reinforce the outside half of the first and last sections with a row of stitching down the gutter (Illus. 111). Use a thin thread for this, such as cotton-covered polyester. You can even sew these stitches by sewing machine if you prefer. For hand sewing, first mark the line $\frac{1}{8}$ inch from the fold and locate stab holes at $\frac{1}{2}$-inch intervals. Stab the holes with an awl. Mark the endpapers (Illus. 110).

ATTACHING TAPES TO THE SEWING BENCH. (Illus. 112–113). Attach the tape to the tape key by wrapping it around the cross bar as shown at B. Slip the taped key sideways

Illus. 106—Having properly folded the endpapers, mark them to the size of the book with trim lines and trim them to size with a straightedge and knife.

Illus. 107—Clamp the book and mark for kettle-stitch sawcuts, $\frac{3}{4}$ inch in from each end. Set a pair of dividers to slightly more than tape width and mark off on the back of the book random locations of up to 4 tapes.

Illus. 108—With square and an ink marker, mark the tape locations with heavy, readily visible lines.

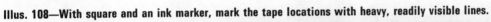

Illus. 109—Saw for kettle-stitches <u>only</u>, no deeper than the inner sheet of each section.

Illus. 110—Position endpapers at both sides of book and mark kettle-stitch and tape locations on the desired fold (see Illus. 99B-C). Do not saw the endpapers.

Illus. 111—Reinforcing stitch for heavy books.

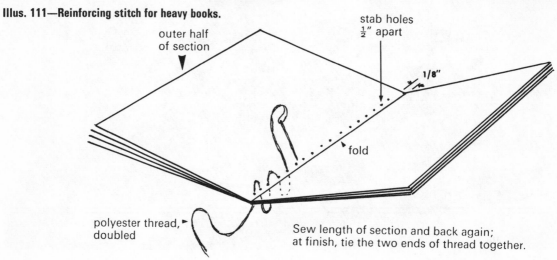

outer half of section

stab holes ½" apart

1/8"

fold

polyester thread, doubled

Sew length of section and back again; at finish, tie the two ends of thread together.

Illus. 112—Place book on a pressing board on the sewing table and use it as a guide for stringing the sewing press with tapes. Extra-long, threaded rods allow the binder to sew several books without stopping. This is called "edition sewing."

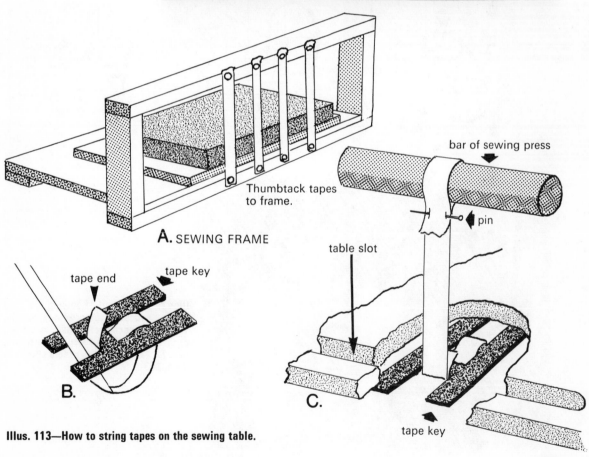

Thumbtack tapes to frame.

A. SEWING FRAME

bar of sewing press

pin

tape end   tape key

table slot

B.

C.

tape key

Illus. 113—How to string tapes on the sewing table.

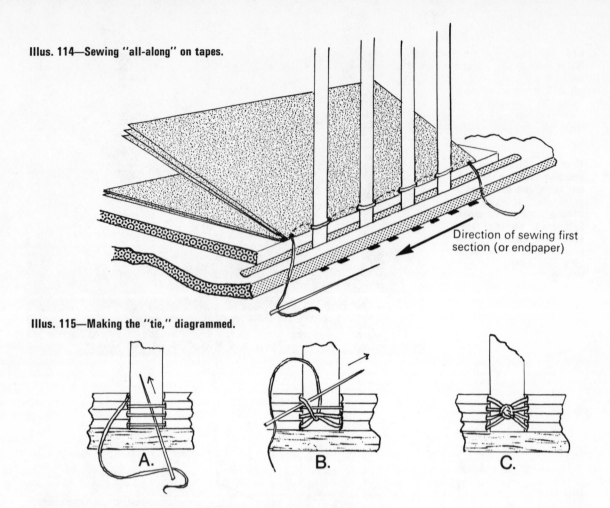

Illus. 114—Sewing "all-along" on tapes.

Direction of sewing first section (or endpaper)

Illus. 115—Making the "tie," diagrammed.

A.

B.

C.

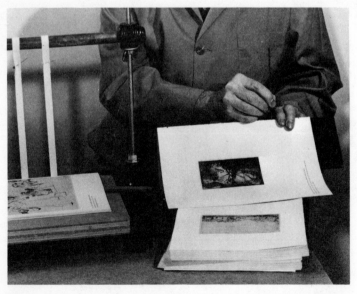

Illus. 116—Instead of sawing the tape marks, you stab them with a needle. You can do each section as it is sewed, or all at once. Use a sharp, heavy needle and, for fast work, the saddle shown in Illus. 203.

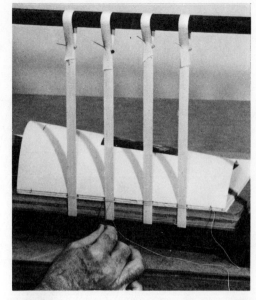

Illus. 117—Sewing is accomplished with the left hand inside the section to pass the needle out at each over-the-tape stitch. Never sew *through* a tape. You have to adjust them after sewing.

through the slot in the table and turn it flat again so as to bear against the underside of the table as shown. Maintain tension on the tape to keep the key from slipping out of its bind, and wrap the tape around the bar from back to front and pin it to itself (Illus. 113C).

When you have strung all the tapes, place a pressing board on the sewing table and the book on top of that, folds of the sections against the tapes (Illus. 112). Line up the tapes with the marks on the back of the book, making sure each tape is vertical; then turn the wing nuts to raise the bar and pull the tapes taut. They

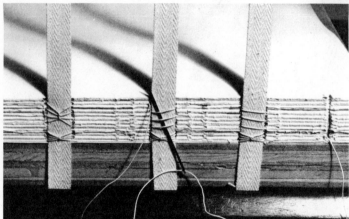

Illus. 118—The first step in making the "tie" is to pass the needle upward between the tape and the previously sewn threads.

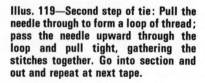

Illus. 119—Second step of tie: Pull the needle through to form a loop of thread; pass the needle upward through the loop and pull tight, gathering the stitches together. Go into section and out and repeat at next tape.

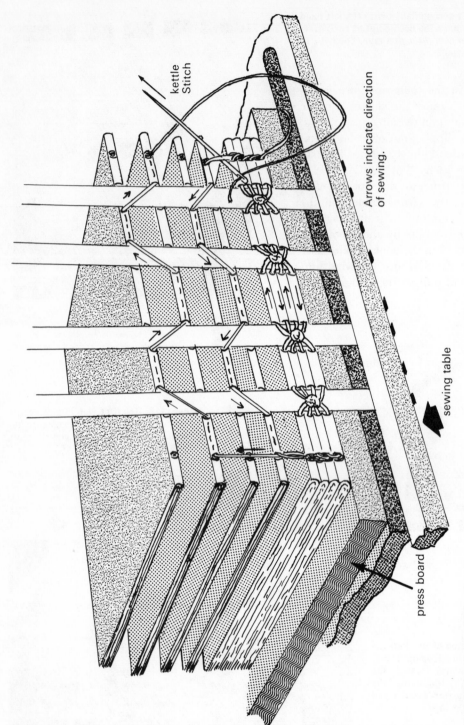

kettle Stitch

Arrows indicate direction
of sewing.

sewing table

press board

Illus. 120—Sewing "off-and-on."

62

Illus. 121—When through sewing, release tension on tapes, remove keys and pull the tapes through until $1\frac{1}{4}$ inches projects below the book. Cut tapes off $1\frac{1}{4}$ inches above the book.

should give off a flat, humming sound when plucked.

Illus. 113A shows how to attach tapes with thumbtacks (drawing pins) to a simple sewing frame. The sewing frame is handy for saving short lengths of tape, which are not long enough for use on the sewing press.

SEWING "ALL-ALONG" ON TAPES. Before sewing each section, you must puncture the fold at each of the tape marks, and you start with the front endpaper (be sure to mark the waste leaf of the endpaper so you know which side goes to the outside of the book).

The endpaper or section may be flattened on a sheet of corrugated cardboard and the fold punctured; or, best is to use the stitching saddle shown in Illus. 203, Chapter 13. This is attached to a corner of the table with a vice or other means and the section can be quickly positioned and accurately punctured (Illus. 116).

Lay the front endpaper waste leaf down on the sewing table, up against the tapes. This puts the head of the book to your right. Pass the needle in through the kettle-stitch puncture, out by the first tape; pass it over the tape and back into the section, receiving the needle there with your left hand. Illus. 114 and 117 show how the length of the section is sewed. The manner of sewing is called "all-along,"

because you sew all along the fold, without skipping a stitch. Never sew *through* a tape, always over it.

Where a book contains 12 or more sections, however, such a manner of sewing can add considerable swell to the back; so, when sewing the fourth section, make a "tie" at each tape to secure the stitches (Illus. 115, 118, 119).

SEWING "OFF-AND-ON." In Illus. 120, the off-and-on manner of sewing is clearly diagrammed. After the first 3 or 4 sections have been sewed all-along, change over to off-and-on, which means that you begin sewing two sections on at once, thus utilizing only half the amount of thread and decreasing the amount of swell that will result from sewing.

Three or more tapes are required in off-and-on sewing. Three tapes are sewed off-and-on in the same way as when sewing on three cords (Illus. 153, Chapter 11). The thread is kettle-stitched at head and tail as in all-along sewing. To keep your place at the middle of the two sections as the needle switches back and forth between them, lay a ruler or long strip of cardboard at the center of each section. It will then be easy to flip the section open to the right place whenever it is to be sewed.

Continue to make the tie every 3 or 4 passes across the book (Illus. 121); then return to sewing all along for the last 3 or 4 sections.

63

When the endpaper is laid on, the waste leaf is on top. Make the tie of preceding stitches while sewing on the endpaper. Finish off the sewing with 2 or 3 kettle stitches, one under the other, and cut off the thread an inch long.

CUTTING DOWN. After sewing, the book is cut down from the sewing table. First relax the tension on the tapes by lowering the bar until the tape keys drop and can be disengaged from the tapes. Pull the tapes upward through the stitches until $1\frac{1}{4}$ inches project below the book. Cut the tapes off with scissors $1\frac{1}{4}$ inches above the book (Illus. 121).

9. Trimming "Out of Boards" and Backing the Tape-Sewn Book

Where a book has a great many sections, as our example book does, and where the paper is a thin, smooth stock, the quantity of thread at the back of the book will make an appreciable difference in thickness between back and fore edge, even after knocking down the swell. A book such as this, though it may be easier to round and back than one that has been able to absorb the swell, presents a problem in trimming the edges. If cut with a guillotine, the book can be padded at front and back with newspaper so that the head and tail can be cut. Lay the paper on, step-fashion, to keep the thickness in balance. When trimming the fore edge, leave the newspaper padding in place to avoid a sloping cut of the fore edge.

TRIMMING OUT OF BOARDS WITH PRESS AND PLOW. The book is said to be trimmed "out of boards" because the boards have not yet been attached and the book has been rounded and backed. If the boards have been attached before trimming, as in the flexibly sewn style (see Chapter 12), the book is said to be "trimmed in boards."

The first step is to jog the book at head and back to straighten up the sections, then paste down the sections (including the endpapers) at the front and back of the book. Leave under a pressing board and weight until the paste dries.

When trimming out of boards, the fore edge must be trimmed first, since it cannot be trimmed after the book has been rounded and backed. Clamp up the book and apply thin, hot, flexible glue to the back, rubbing it well in between the folds. (If Elmer's Glue-All is used, be sure to spread it on *thinly*.)

TYING UP THE BOOK. (Illus. 122). Hold the book firmly to keep it from falling out of shape and wrap several turns of tape around it and tuck in the end as shown in the drawing. The tape holds the book in shape for trimming. Lay the book on the back cutting board with a cardboard between book and board; then lay on the front cutting board, even with the trim line. Insert in the press in the usual way and trim the fore edge with the plow.

Owing to the extra-thick swell at the back, the head and tail cannot be cut in the usual manner, so trimming must wait until after the book has been rounded and backed. This is done as has already been described, after

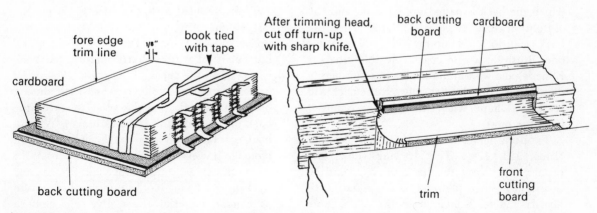

Illus. 122—Tie up book for trimming fore edge "out of boards."

Illus. 123—Book in press for trimming head "out of boards."

Illus. 124—After the head has been trimmed, the fold at the turn-up remains uncut. Cut off with long-bladed knife, such as this butcher knife.

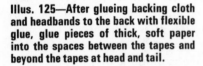

Illus. 125—After glueing backing cloth and headbands to the back with flexible glue, glue pieces of thick, soft paper into the spaces between the tapes and beyond the tapes at head and tail.

which the back is pasted up, let soak, and the old glue scraped away with a knife. Wipe the back clean with a damp rag, followed by a dry one. Brush on a thin coat of flexible glue (or Elmer's) and wait until the glue has thoroughly dried. When the glue has fully set, the back will retain its shape when the book is removed from the press.

TRIMMING HEAD AND TAIL OUT OF BOARDS. (Illus. 123, 124). The drawing shows the proper way to set the book between cutting boards (of $\frac{1}{4}$-inch plywood or tempered hardboard) and to position it in the press. Note that the cutting boards do *not* extend beyond the turn-up formed in backing the book.

Trim the head in the usual way. When the last leaf has been cut, a small fold at the turn-up remains still uncut. Do not tear this away, but cut it off with a sharp, long-bladed knife lying flat on the cheek of the press (Illus. 124).

BACKING CLOTH. Super, which has already been introduced, may be used to cover the back of the book and serve as hinges. When a book is as large and heavy as the demonstration model, however (it measures $9 \times 12 \times 1\frac{1}{2}$ inches thick), a stronger hinge will be obtained by using a backing cloth of unbleached muslin or similar material. First give the cloth a light-to-medium starching with spray starch, or prepared liquid starch. Iron it dry.

66

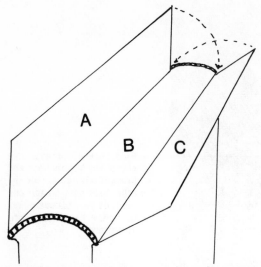

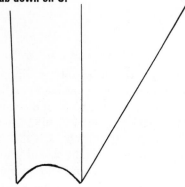

Illus. 126—The hollow back: Glue B to back of book; fold C over B and brush glue on surface. Fold A over and rub down on C.

Glue the backing cloth down over the tapes, rubbing it down well between the tapes to prevent lifting. Since the bulges made by the tapes would be unsightly if allowed to show through the cloth spine, you must "fill in between the tapes."

FILLING IN. (Illus. 125). Cut a strip of soft, thick paper, such as heavy drawing paper, the same width as the back, as measured over the curve. Cut the strip into lengths that will fit in between the tapes as well as beyond the tapes at head and tail.

Illus. 127—The book in a bench press. Rub the center section of the hollow back with a bone folder until well adhered.

Cut headbands and glue them in place at head and tail. If you prefer, you can make the hand-sewn headbands described in Chapter 13.

Brush glue over the backs of the headbands and in the spaces to be filled. Position the pieces of paper and rub them down to adhere them as in Illus. 125.

THE HOLLOW BACK. In a previous demonstration, as well as in publishers' editions in general, the hollow back consists simply of a strip of paper glued over the backing cloth and a corresponding strip glued inside the cover material. Sometimes the strip over the backing cloth is omitted, but it is better to include it.

To make a good, solid book, use the folded hollow back (Illus. 126, 127, 128). Take a piece of heavy kraft paper; or, better, singleply Bristol board (which is called "card" in England) with a kid finish. Cut a piece three times the width of the back and long enough to cover the back from the outer edge of one headband to the outer edge of the other.

Divide the width into thirds and fold the side thirds over the middle one. The grain must run parallel to the folds. Then glue up the back with flexible glue and lay the center panel in place and rub it down with the folder. Then, fold down one or the other of the two remaining sides over the back and brush with glue. Finally, bring down the third division upon the section and rub it into contact.

Another method of treatment is to leave the third section of the hollow back considerably

Illus. 128—Fold over one side of the hollow back and brush it with glue. Fold the other side over on top and rub it down. This completes the hollow back. Leave until glue dries.

wider than the back. When the hollow back has been entirely glued, this excess projects beyond the book. When the glue has dried, fold the excess upward against a metal ruler and crease it, then cut off by running a sharp knife along the crease.

In regard to the glue for this, a cold, liquid hide glue that has been made flexible by the addition of glycerine is recommended, particularly in the last glueing stage. It is essential that the folded-over section be able to slip on the glued section so that the hollow back can be fitted tightly to the back of the book. If the glue takes hold too quickly, you will not have enough time to brush the entire back before it starts to set up, and, as a result, it will grab at the most inopportune moment, so that you may have to tear the hollow off the back and start over.

10. Boarding and Covering the Tape-Sewn Book

As a binder you have a choice of using "plain" boards or "split" boards. Plain boards are simply glued to the super tabs. Split boards are described below. Buckram has been chosen for cover material in this demonstration in order to explain the treatment involved.

SPLIT BOARDS. What has been said before in regard to boards holds equally good here. However, for a stronger, higher quality construction, we shall use split boards.

A split board is made by glueing together a thick board and a thin sheet of cardboard or pulpboard (strawboard in England). Cut the boards oversize with perfectly straight back edges. Mark a line down each thick board 2 inches from the back edge. Brush glue over the entire board, up to this line. Lay on the thin cardboard and rub it down, making sure the back edges are even with each other. Glue up two such boards and put them between waxed paper in the press. Apply heavy pressure. The two boards are thus glued solidly together except for the 2-inch-wide strip down the back edge, which is open or split. Trim the boards to size by cutting off the excess cardboard at head, tail and fore edge.

On the other hand, if the book you are binding is a small or lightweight book, the extra strength of the split board is not needed, and you may use simply a single board.

THE TAB. The tab consists of the backing cloth, the tapes, and a small part of the waste leaf (Illus. 129–131). Cut both waste leaves out around the backing cloth as shown, then slip a sheet of newspaper under the tab and glue the cloth and tapes directly to the paper tab.

BOARDING WITH A SINGLE-THICKNESS BOARD. This is simple. Just place the back edge of the board on the glued tab (the newspaper having been replaced by a piece of waxed paper), adjust it for the correct width of groove and the correct square at head and tail. Lay the board down flat on the board paper and repeat with

Illus. 129—Mark around the backing cloth on the waste leaf, making a tab a little wider and a little longer than the overhang of cloth. Cut out with scissors.

Illus. 130 — Protect the board paper with newspaper and brush hard glue on the tab, under and over the tapes and backing cloth. Note split board at left.

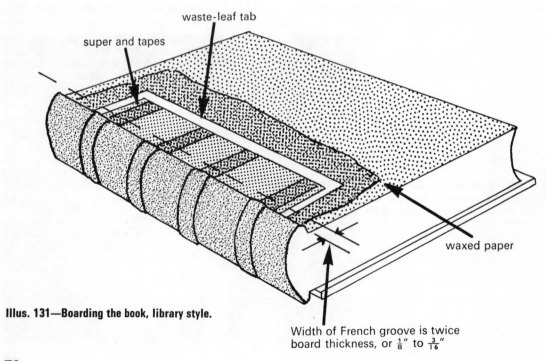

waste-leaf tab

super and tapes

waxed paper

Illus. 131—Boarding the book, library style.

Width of French groove is twice board thickness, or $\frac{1}{8}$″ to $\frac{3}{16}$″

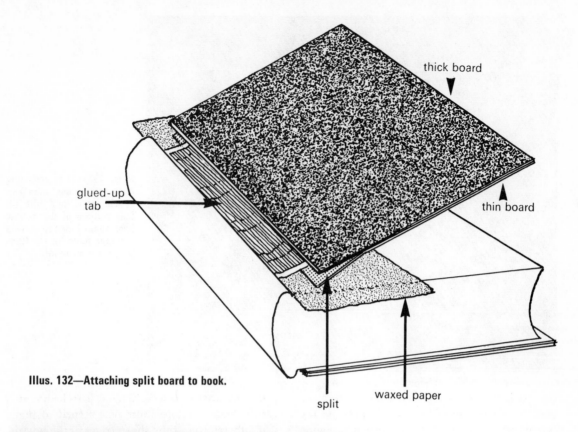

thick board

glued-up tab

thin board

Illus. 132—Attaching split board to book.

split

waxed paper

Illus. 133—Note waxed paper between book and grooving boards to prevent sticking. Also observe that the traditional—and expensive—handwheel of the standing press has been replaced by three equally efficient steel bars, less expensive. The bars are wedged into holes drilled through the walls of the nut and into the body of the press screw. Always center the book under the press screw.

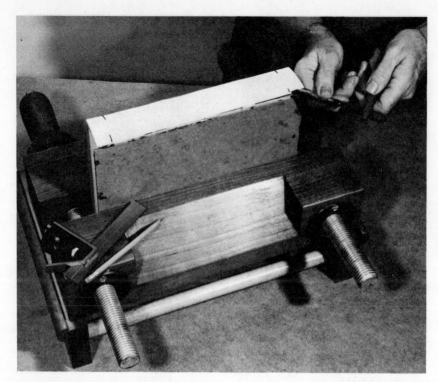

Illus. 134—After removing book from press, clamp in bench press and slit all four corners of the hollow back about $\frac{7}{8}$ inch deep. This provides room for the turn-in of cover material.

the other board. Wrap waxed paper over the book while holding it firmly to prevent the boards from slipping. Place between grooving boards and press until the next day (Illus. 133).

BOARDING WITH SPLIT BOARDS. When boarding with split boards, the thin board in every case goes against the book.

After glueing up the tab (Illus. 130), open the split in the board and brush it with hard glue, either hot glue, liquid glue or Elmer's, but the same glue you used on the tab.

Lift the tab and insert it in the split of the board, which you then bring down on the tab to the correct width of groove and the correct square at head and tail (Illus. 132). Rub the board down along the back edge, then carefully turn the book over and attach the other split board. Put the book to press between grooving boards, with waxed paper between the jaws and the groove. Apply maximum pressure and leave the book until the next day (Illus. 133).

THE BUCKRAM COVER. "Library buckram," as it is called, is a heavy, linen cloth, available in a number of colors. Since it is so heavy, it is stiff, and therefore must be softened to make it adhere around the sharp edges of the boards.

Upon removing the book from press, the first step is to slit all 4 corners of the hollow back for the turn-in (Illus. 134).

To measure for the cover, wrap a long strip of paper around the book (Illus. 135), crease where the edges of the boards come, then measure the strip from crease to crease and add $1\frac{1}{2}$ inches plus twice the board thickness for turn-in. In the same way, you determine the width of the cover material by taking the height of the boards and adding $1\frac{1}{2}$ inches plus twice the board thickness. Remember in laying out the cover that the height of the book runs parallel to the selvedge.

PASTING ON WITH NON-WARPING PASTE. Non-warping paste is manufactured without water and therefore does not cause warping when it dries. If you are using this kind of paste, brush it all over the inside of the buckram, then fold the latter over upon itself and let it soak for 5 minutes. Then open out

Illus. 135—How to measure the book for its cover. Wrap a paper strip around as shown, bend it upwards at the bottom and downwards at the top. Measure distance from crease to crease and add 1½ inches plus twice the thickness of the board for turn-in.

Illus. 136—Rub the paste-softened buckram into the French groove with the edge of a folder. Use a damp rag in the other hand to wipe up paste smears. Rub the cover down all over with the edge of the folder.

the buckram and paste it up again; fold it over on itself and let soak 5 minutes. Open out and paste up a third time and the cover is ready to go on the book.

Position the book on the pasted side at one end and bring the buckram over the book and rub it down (Illus. 136).

In the library style of binding (where the boards are first glued to the book) a problem arises in tucking the turn-in of the cover under

Illus. 137—Hold book by its body and let the boards drop open. Turn in the near side of the cover as shown. Push it under the headband with your free hand, then use the folder to rub it down under the back, as well as along the edges of the boards.

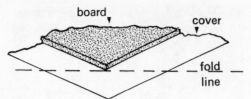

A. Open boards on glued cover.

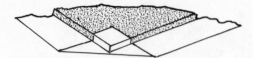

B. Fold corner cloth over board.

Illus. 138—The "library corner."

C. Fold over cloth at head and tail.

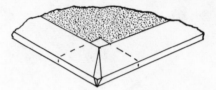

D. Fold over cloth at fore edges.

the headbands (Illus. 137). If you have a second person present, he or she might hold the book upright, leaving you with both hands free to tuck the turn-in into place where it passes under the headband and over the paper of the hollow back. Or, you can support a bench press or the glueing clamp 3 or 4 inches above the table and clamp the body of the book in the end (Illus. 231, Chapter 13). Or, you can try to become skilled enough to perform the operation single-handed, as shown. In any case, the buckram must be turned in under the headbands, passing through the slits cut at the four corners of the hollow back. Then rub the buckram into good contact with the paper hollow and crease its folded edge with a folder (Illus. 137).

When both head and tail have been turned in under headband and tailband, consider making the "library corner" (Illus. 138). This is the type of corner you will find on buckram-bound books at the public library. It gives the corner of the board a high degree of protection and is exceptionally resistant to wear. It has one fault, however. The multiplex folds of cover material thicken the corners. To reduce this thickness as much as possible, use a pair of band nippers, or any wide-nosed, flat-jawed pliers to squeeze the corner flat (Illus. 139). If the jaws are serrated, either file them smooth

Illus. 139—To reduce the bulk of the library corner, squeeze gently between smooth jaws of band nippers or wide-nose, flat-jaw pliers. Glass-breaking pliers are shown.

or cover with thin manila or sheet aluminum, held on with transparent tape, or with two thicknesses of masking tape.

The corners are completed by turning in the fore edges. Rub the turn-in all round to adhere it, and if difficulty is encountered anywhere, lift the buckram and repaste. Close the boards and rub down the outside, pushing the buckram on each side toward and over the edges. Sharpen the edges further by rubbing with the folder and see to it that the excess cloth is pushed over the edge and inside the

Illus. 140—With book in press between grooving boards, shape, flatten and smooth the cover at head and tail, using a pointed folder.

Illus. 141—Mark the turn-in for trimming. With dividers, set off a space $\frac{3}{8}$ inch wide all around; mark inner limit of turn-in by punching with sharp point of dividers.

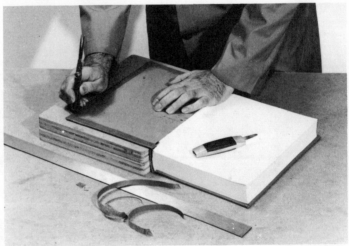

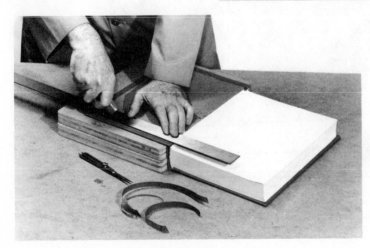

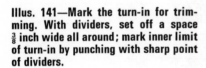

Illus. 142—Trim out excess turn-in, using a sharp knife and a steel straight-edge.

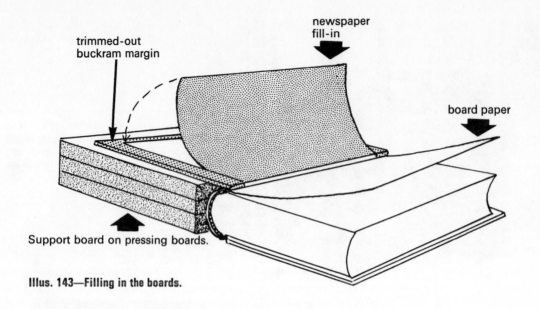

trimmed-out
buckram margin

newspaper
fill-in

board paper

Support board on pressing boards.

Illus. 143—Filling in the boards.

FLEXIBLE
NON-WARPING
PASTE

Illus. 144—Pasting the board paper. Brush paste thoroughly into the groove at the hinge. Use the same paste on the board paper that was used on the buckram cover.

boards. Rub it down well so that it will not lift in the squares.

Slip a sheet of flashing aluminum or 3-ply Bristol board (card) between book and boards and place in press under heavy pressure. Take a pointed folder and shape the corners of the back (Illus. 140). Leave until the next day.

Upon taking the book out of press, open the front board and support it on a pile of pressing boards. Mark the turn-in and trim it out (Illus. 141–142). Also trim out the end board.

Protect the book with newspaper and brush paste all over the board paper. Close the board on the book, then open it and rub down the board paper with your hand. Paste down the other board paper the same way. But remember —if non-warping paste is used on the outside of the board, the same paste *must* be used inside.

Slip a sheet of waxed paper between each board and the book and press until the following day.

PASTING ON WITH WATER-BASE PASTE. The formula given on page 157 makes a very good grade of paste out of flour and water.

The only difference is that the introduction of water into the scheme of things causes a slight problem. When using this paste, the buckram cover will exert more of a pull on the board than will the board paper. In consequence, the boards will warp outward and you will have to paste down a second board paper over the first to equalize the pull and straighten out the board.

FILLING IN THE BOARDS. (Illus. 143). Therefore, after trimming out the boards, cut a piece of plain newsprint (or printed newspaper, it makes no difference) slightly smaller than the open area of the board. Brush paste on the newspaper fill-in and rub it down inside the board. The moisture will cause it to stretch and fill the space. Treat both boards the same way and press with waxed paper under the boards to prevent the moisture from cockling the pages of the book.

The following day, remove the book from press and paste down the board papers as described above (Illus. 144) and press 24 hours. Be sure that the paste you use on the board papers is the same as was used on the cover.

Illus. 145—The demonstration model, an old book picked up at a second-hand bookstore. It is quarter bound in red cloth with printed paper siding and hand-sewed on three cords.

Illus. 146—The first step in tearing down a hard-cover book is to slice through the hinges on both sides. (Note buried cords.)

Illus. 147—Peel old padding off the back. With a book as old as this one, the glue crumbles and is easily scraped away without pasting the back to soften it.

11. Sewing on Buried Cords
Quarter Binding in Leather with False Bands

As late as the end of the 19th century, books were still being sewed on cords by hand. The cord-sewn book is both strong and flexible and will lie flat when opened.

TEARING DOWN. Tearing down a book with hard covers differs from tearing down a paperback only in the manner of removing the covers. You must first cut through the hinge on both sides (Illus. 146), then tear off and discard the flyleaf attached to each side of the book.

Also, the back of a hard-cover book is likely to have a certain amount of padding, including super, and this must be carefully torn off (Illus. 147). Scrape off the old glue—if necessary, soak it with paste first to soften it.

THE OLD BOARDS. Sometimes the old boards can be saved and used again. Strip the cover material off the outside and scrape away the board paper. If it is reluctant to give up, dampen it with a sponge.

If the corners have been bruised so that they are soft and separated into layers or laminations, brush *hard* glue in among the laminations, squeeze out the excess, and let dry under a weighted board with waxed paper on either side to prevent sticking.

When dry, cut the boards down to the correct size for the trimmed book.

KNOCKING OUT THE GROOVE. When the book is torn down, the turned-up folds tend to keep their shape, and flattening them is called "knocking out the groove."

Take several sections at a time and hammer along the folds with a plastic-faced mallet or similar tool (Illus. 148). Do this on the knocking-down block gripped in the lying press. Turn the sections over and hammer down the other side. Do this several times until the folds are as flattened as they will get.

PRESSING THE SECTIONS. Assemble the sections back edge to fore edge and press under heavy pressure until the following day.

"MADE" ENDPAPERS. While the sections are

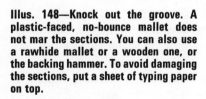
Illus. 148—Knock out the groove. A plastic-faced, no-bounce mallet does not mar the sections. You can also use a rawhide mallet or a wooden one, or the backing hammer. To avoid damaging the sections, put a sheet of typing paper on top.

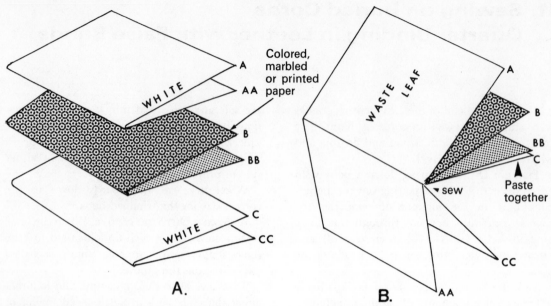

Illus. 149—Construction of "made" endpapers.

pressing, you can be getting the endpapers ready (Illus. 149). These are called "made" endpapers because they are made by pasting two leaves together. Cut the sheets oversize; you can trim them to size later. When you have pasted the endpapers together, give them a hard squeeze in the press, then put them aside under a pressing board and weight to dry.

The leaves designated "colored" (B-BB) may be commercially available colored paper, such as a pastel paper; they can be printed with an overall pattern; or, you can print them yourself with a linoleum block or wood cut, using the screw press (Chapter 14).

To tint your own paper, soak it in a bath of water to which acrylic tube paint has been added. When it is thoroughly soaked, drain the paper and hang it up to dry. This will cause it to cockle (pucker) out of shape, so soak it again in plain water and dry it between blotters, under a board and weight to keep the whole thing flat. Acrylic colors are waterproof when dry, so you need not fear the colors running. If you change the blotters every few hours, the colored papers will be ready for use the next day.

Illus. 149B shows proper assembly of the sheets. For extra strength, paste a strip $\frac{1}{8}$ inch wide along the fold of CC, on the outside, so that, when assembled, CC will be pasted by this strip to AA. Rub down with a folder for good adhesion.

SAWING THE BACK FOR BURIED CORDS. (Illus. 150). First make sure all the sections are in proper order and that none is upside down. Clamp the book up for sawing the back. (The demonstration example required no sawing, as the original saw cuts were used.)

Three cords are enough for a book up to 8vo (6×9 inches) in size. A larger book may have as many as 5, the outside limit.

Saw in the kettle-stitch cuts as at B in the drawing. The cord cuts, however, are to be wider at the bottom to accommodate the bulk of the cord, so tilt the saw blade from side to side as indicated at A. Saw just deep enough to penetrate the fold of the innermost sheet of each section.

After sawing, position the endpapers and mark the folds for puncturing with a needle before sewing.

80

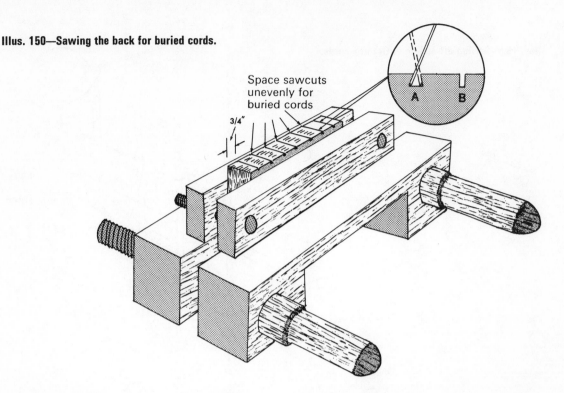

Space sawcuts
unevenly for
buried cords

3/4"

A   B

STRINGING THE TABLE WITH CORDS. (Illus. 151). Cut the cord into as many lengths as needed. Figures A and B show how the cord takes a friction grip around the neck of the cord key. The keys may be cut from $\frac{1}{16}$-inch-thick brass, copper or aluminum, or from $\frac{1}{4}$-inch hardwood or plywood.

Each cord will require a "lay cord" (Illus. 151C), which is a loop of cord tied around the sewing table bar. You should make all the loops as nearly the same size as possible.

To string a cord, slip it edgewise through the slot in the table, maintaining constant tension on the cord, and bring it up to bear against

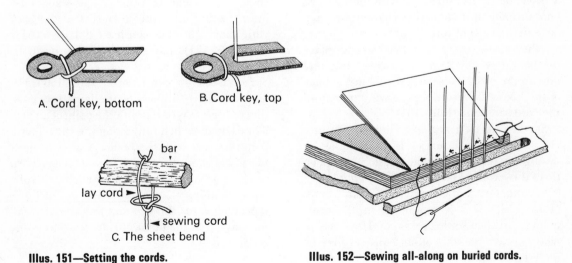

A. Cord key, bottom

B. Cord key, top

bar

lay cord ▶

◀ sewing cord

C. The sheet bend

Illus. 151—Setting the cords.

Illus. 152—Sewing all-along on buried cords.

81

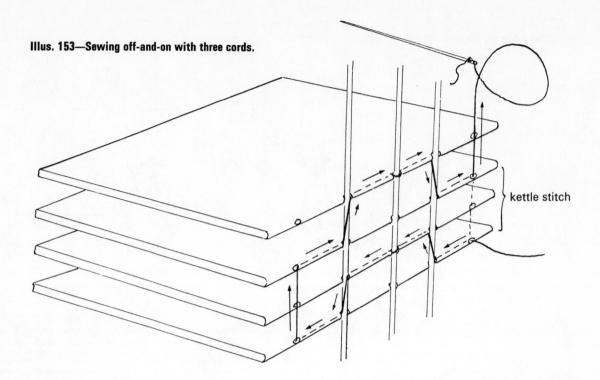

Illus. 153—Sewing off-and-on with three cords.

kettle stitch

the underside of the table. Pass the upper end of the cord through the loop of the lay cord and pull it downwards until tight. Hold the cords between thumb and forefinger while you then pass the end of the cord around the loop and back underneath itself. Pull tight. When used in this fashion, the knot just made is called a "sheet bend." It is identical with the weaver's knot introduced in an earlier chapter for tying on a new length of thread.

When all the cords have been strung, place the book face down on the sewing table and line up the cords with the saw cuts in the back of the book. Then turn up the wing nuts until the cords are taut (Illus. 154).

SEWING ALL-ALONG ON BURIED CORDS. (Illus. 152). The technique is the same as for sewing on tapes, except that you do not make a tie of the sewing thread every few sections.

SEWING OFF-AND-ON WITH BURIED CORDS. (Illus. 153). This is conducted in the same manner as when sewing on tapes. However, in neither case should off-and-on sewing be undertaken with fewer than three cords or

tapes. The drawing shows graphically how the sewing is equalized among the three cords.

FORWARDING. Continue with forwarding the book by pulling through the cords until $1\frac{1}{4}$ inches project below, then cut them off to the same measure above the book (Illus. 155).

Round and back the book and trim the edges (in whichever order circumstances require), and glue on headbands. Pad the back with super and the constructed hollow back (see Illus. 127). Lay the book aside until the glue sets.

FRAYING OUT THE CORDS. (Illus. 156–157). To avoid both stiffness of the joint and bulk, the cords are frayed out with the point of an awl. This is done by first untwisting the end of cord, then raking it with the point. A piece of sheet metal will protect the book from damage. Then scrape out the ends with the rounded point of a knife, thinning them so that the fan of fibres tapers outwards. Loosen and fray the cords all the way up to the point of emergence from the book.

82

Illus. 154—The sewing table set up with three cords. The long (18 inches) side-screws allow edition binding—that is, sewing several books before cutting down. Saddle gripped in vice at extreme left makes puncturing endpapers easy and accurate. Note needle in small hand vice for easier handling.

Illus. 155—After sewing, the book is cut down. The cords are pulled through until 1¼ inches project below the book. Cut off.

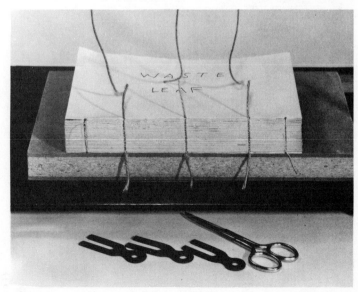

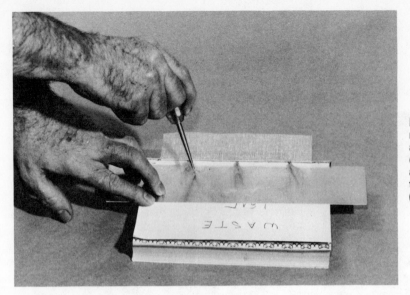

Illus. 156—The book has been rounded and backed and the super and hollow back glued on. Fray out the cords with an awl against a piece of sheet metal to protect the book. Thin out excess fibres. (Note printed endpapers.)

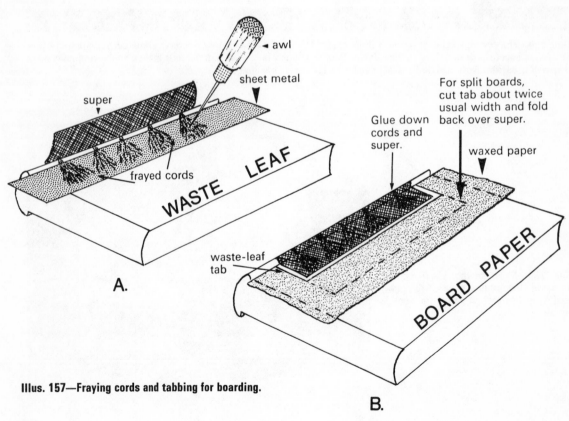

Illus. 157—Fraying cords and tabbing for boarding.

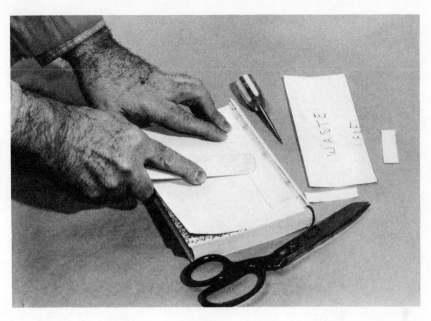

Illus. 158—Folding back the paper tab for split boards. Note that folded-back edge falls short of turn-up to allow for the French groove.

MAKING THE TAB. (Illus. 157B, 158). For a single-thickness board, cut the tab out of the waste leaf slightly larger than the super hinge.

For split boards, cut the paper tab approximately twice as wide, fold the excess back over the super and crease it with a folder (Illus. 158). Fold the paper back only to where the back edge of the board will come in forming the French groove, and not all the way back to the turn-up.

Make split boards as described in Chapter 10.

BOARDING. Slip newspaper under the tab and brush glue over the waste-leaf tab. Press the cords and super down into the glue, then brush more glue over them. Fold the excess paper back over the super and rub it down.

Open the split of the board and brush in cold, liquid glue. Slip the split over the tab to the edge of the turned-back paper. Remove the newspaper, insert a sheet of waxed paper, and bring the board down on the book. Set the squares and check the fore edge overhang, then rub the board down on the inserted tab.

Turn the book over and attach the other board in the same way. Wrap waxed paper around the book, place it between grooving boards and press under heavy pressure until the next day.

Whenever you insert a book in the press, always check it by viewing it on a level from all angles to make sure nothing has gone askew. If a book is crooked in the press, it will remain so when removed, and it will have to be torn down and started over.

FALSE BANDS. Although the book may be covered with a smooth back if desired, there is an old-fashioned charm about a book with bands decorating the back. Modern publishers' bindings often fake the bands by printing an appearance of them with gold lines.

False bands add nothing to the book except appearance. They are an imitation of the *real* bands which appear and are an integral part of the book structure when it is sewed on outside cords (Chap. 12).

First, make the hollow back with 5 cross-lines for band locations. Spaces between bands are narrower towards the head of the book, as the upper ones carry the title and the author's name.

Illus. 159 shows how the bands are cut with sloping sides and glued into place on the hollow back. To get leather thick enough, two pieces may be glued together, then cut into strips. A very good source of band material is a leather boot lace (Illus. 160). Cut the bands

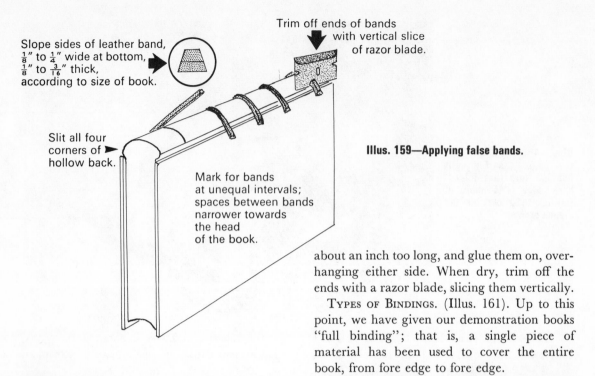

Slope sides of leather band, $\frac{1}{8}"$ to $\frac{1}{4}"$ wide at bottom, $\frac{1}{8}"$ to $\frac{3}{16}"$ thick, according to size of book.

Trim off ends of bands with vertical slice of razor blade.

Slit all four corners of hollow back.

Illus. 159—Applying false bands.

Mark for bands at unequal intervals; spaces between bands narrower towards the head of the book.

about an inch too long, and glue them on, overhanging either side. When dry, trim off the ends with a razor blade, slicing them vertically.

TYPES OF BINDINGS. (Illus. 161). Up to this point, we have given our demonstration books "full binding"; that is, a single piece of material has been used to cover the entire book, from fore edge to fore edge.

Illus. 160—Trimming the bands, which were cut from boot lace in foreground. The book shown is an example of a quarter-binding with false bands and paper siding. It is sewed on three buried cords, the ends of which are laced into the board (see Chapter 12).

The quarter binding (Illus. 161A) features a back of one kind of material and a siding of another.

There are two types of half binding—with corners or with a trim the length of the fore edge as at B and C. Books with corners are seldom seen any more, except for large blank books such as ledgers. The fore edge trim, however, is becoming increasingly popular, books often having back and fore edge of cloth (where the greatest wear comes), while the siding is of paper.

SHARPENING STONES. (Illus. 162). The knives and blades you use for cutting paper and leather should be kept as keen-edged as possible. A dull knife will tear and spoil material.

Many kinds of sharpening stones are available, but the best are the world-famous Arkansas stones, made from a mineral found near Hot Springs, Arkansas, U.S.A. The mineral is called "novaculite," derived from the Latin word for razor. Three grades of

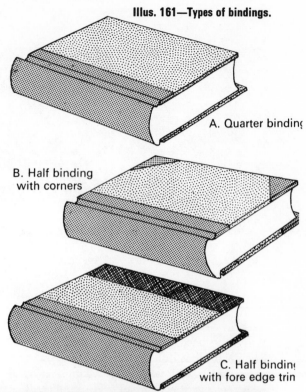

Illus. 161—Types of bindings.

A. Quarter binding

B. Half binding with corners

C. Half binding with fore edge trim

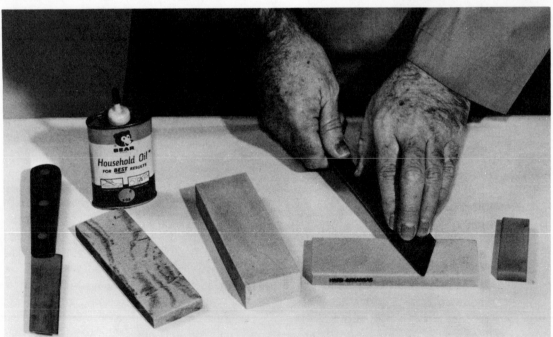

Illus. 162—Keep your knives and leather-paring tools sharp with Arkansas stones. Left to right: Washita stone, soft Arkansas stone, hard Arkansas stone; hard Arkansas engraver's slip for honing the plow knife.

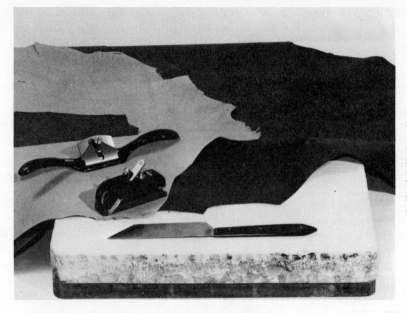

Illus. 163—The gray skin is suede sheep, the two darker hides are red and tan morocco. Tools (foreground to background): German-style leather-paring knife; bull-nose rabbet plane; spokeshave. The paring stone is a lithographic stone. A marble slab or plate glass can also be used.

coarseness or density occur. The coarsest is the Washita stone, suitable for fast sharpening when a blade is dull. Next is the *soft* Arkansas stone which will whet a jack-knife, carving tools, etc., to the point of serviceability. The finest grained stone of all is called *hard* Arkansas stone, and this provides the keenest edge of all. After an edge has been ground and whetted on the first two stones, it is honed on the last one. If a leather strop is available, it is good to finish the edge on this, drawing the blade across the leather with the edge trailing so as to remove the slight burr resulting from stoning.

Hard Arkansas oil stone is used to sharpen surgical instruments, wood and metal engraving tools, etc. However, the Arkansas stones are relatively expensive and, where cost is a factor, a combination (coarse on one side, fine on the other) India oil stone, or a Crystolon or Carborundum stone (both are silicon carbide) is recommended.

Use plenty of oil and grind and hone the knife blades on both sides. The leather paring knife is sharpened only on the bevelled side, never on the flat side, which may be drawn a few times over a leather strop to remove the burr. When sharpening a plane or spokeshave

blade (see Illus. 163), make sure the bevel rides flat on the stone. Do not stone the flat side, except gently on a very fine oil stone (hard Arkansas or a razor hone) or leather strop to remove the burr. When you are through using an oil stone, always wipe it clean and dry it before putting it away.

LEATHER. Bookbinding leathers are made for that express purpose and may consist of cowhide, calfskin, pigskin, sheepskin, goatskin, etc. (Illus. 163). The preferred leather is morocco, a type of goatskin that is tanned in a special way to create durability and a handsomely grained surface. It is available in colors. The best morocco is stamped on the flesh side: MANUFACTURED IN ENGLAND.

Bookbinding leathers, as sold by bookbinders' supply houses, consist of a whole skin priced by the square foot—at a rate of about 10 times the cost of buckram. However, you may be able to find in your own locality a leather shop that sells scraps, sometimes called "findings." Also, hobby shops sell leather for various kinds of leatherwork, among which you may find something suitable for covering a book. This may not be the best of leather for bookbinding, professionally speaking, but it will certainly do and it may pay you to look

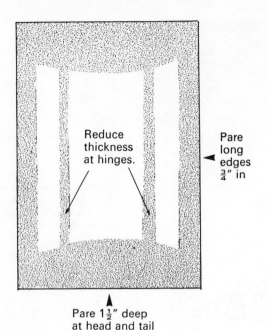

Reduce
thickness
at hinges.

Pare
long
edges
¾" in

Pare 1½" deep
at head and tail

Illus. 164—Paring leather for a quarter binding.

The morocco skins shown in Illus. 163 contain about 9 square feet apiece. The sheep contains 5 square feet.

CUTTING OUT THE LEATHER. Mark a line down the length of each board, parallel to the back edge and 1 inch removed from it. Wrap a strip of paper around the back of the book, over a band, and mark where it intersects each of the two lines. Measure from mark to mark and add ¼ inch to get the width of leather needed for the back. The length of the piece will be equal to the height of the boards plus 2 inches, which allows an inch at head and tail for turning in, also accommodating the board thickness.

Mark out the piece on the flesh side of the leather and cut it out with a straightedge and a knife.

LEATHER WORKING TOOLS. Leather used for bookbinding has to have its edges pared and sometimes it must be thinned. The leather-paring knife (Illus. 163 and 165) is a fast, efficient tool in the hands of a skilled operator. It does not co-operate so readily with the un-

around. A piece of black horsehide cut from such a scrap was used by the author in 1939 to quarter bind a book. The binding is still in excellent condition, save for a little normal wear on the edges.

Illus. 165—Using the leather paring knife. Keep angle of knife as shallow as possible. Too steep an angle causes the blade to cut through the leather.

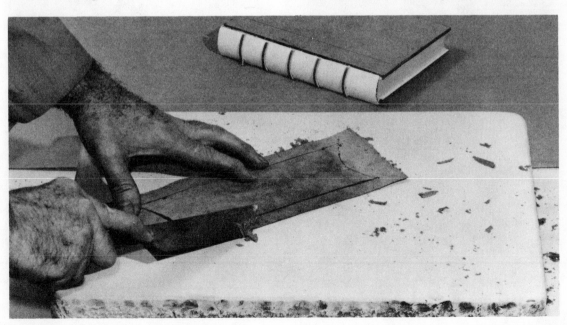

Illus. 166—The Stanley bull-nose rabbet plane thins edges, removes any "bumpiness" left by the knife.

Illus. 167—Using the spokeshave to thin leather that is too thick. Clamp one end of leather as shown; pull spoke-shave toward you, using both hands. Reverse leather under clamp and plane down the other end.

90

skilled user. Often, it will leave a bumpy surface, and this must be smoothed out. The Stanley bull-nose rabbet plane (Illus. 163 and 166) is barely 4 inches long, but it can follow after the knife and smooth out the sloping bevel that the knife has given the edge. The plane can even replace the knife, since the blade is located at the front end of the tool, where it can shave off the edge in a sloping manner, a feat that is more difficult for the plane that has its blade located farther back toward the center of the tool.

When the back of the book is provided with bands, the leather there must be somewhat thinner than if the back were smooth. Where leather has to be removed over a flat area, the spokeshave (Illus. 167) can be used as illustrated. A block plane is also a good leather thinner, even the $3\frac{1}{2}$-inch plane with a 1-inch blade. A larger one is more efficient, however, and the Stanley 6-inch block plane with blade at a 20° angle, or the Stanley low-angle (12°) block plane, is particularly recommended. Both of these planes are minutely adjustable with an adjusting wheel, making it easy to adjust the blade to the thinnest possible cut. Both planes also have a moveable shoe at the front of the sole plate which should be adjusted to provide the narrowest possible throat opening in front of the blade. Where the high angle blade cuts smoothly, the low-angle blade cuts faster.

PARING THE LEATHER. Not all leather requires the same amount of paring, and some is so thin that it does not need paring at all. However, a leather such as morocco requires its edges pared to a feather edge with the leather-paring knife (Illus. 165) and/or the bull-nosed rabbet plane. Mark where the hinges come (Illus. 164) and pare a little off the thickness with the heel of the knife or the bull-nose rabbet plane held at an angle to the line of paring. Keep blowing or brushing the parings away, so that none gets under the leather. If one should, it would make a bump, causing the knife to shear completely through the leather.

For a quarter or half binding, pare the long edges of the leather $\frac{3}{4}$ inch in. When using the plane, adjust the blade for the thinnest possible cut. If the plane alone is used, it will take longer than paring with the knife, but it will do a good job. It is especially good for paring down the ends of the leather, which should be pared quite thin for about 2 inches in from each end (twice the amount of the turn-in), since it is here that the leather is turned over on itself on the back of the book (Illus. 166).

A lithographic stone is the traditional paring stone on which the leather paring takes place (Illus. 163), but current high prices put such a stone out of the reach of most amateurs. Still and all, you can do just as well with a 1-inch-thick slab of marble from a stone yard, about 11×14 inches in size; or use a piece of $\frac{1}{4}$-inch-thick plate that has had its sharp edges ground off.

Whenever you use a plane or a spokeshave on leather, always adjust the blade for the lightest possible cut and do not bear down on the tool. Take the spokeshave by both handles and draw it toward you with a slight tilt forward (Illus. 167).

PASTING THE LEATHER. Although it is possible to use the commercial variety of non-warping paste with leather, particularly if the back is to be smooth (without bands), the flour paste made with water is preferred (see formula on page 157). The paste made with water soaks and softens the leather better and makes it more tractable when rubbing up the bands.

Lay the leather flesh side up on a piece of newspaper and brush it generously with paste. Fold it over on itself and let it soak for about 5 minutes, then spread it out and paste it up again. If the leather feels soft and loose, it is ready to go on the back of the book. If any stiffness remains, fold the leather over on itself and let it soak another 5 minutes, then open it out, brush on some more paste, smooth it out with your fingers, removing lumps, and apply it to the back of the book.

BAND STICKS. These are foot-long sticks of birch, maple, or other hardwood, with ends about $\frac{13}{16}$-inch square (Illus. 169). The grooves

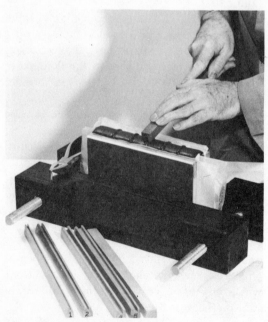

are made with a dado saw and are $\frac{1}{4}$ inch deep. The width is supposed to just fit over the band being rubbed up. When making your own band sticks, groove them as follows: $\frac{3}{32}''$, $\frac{1}{8}''$, $\frac{3}{16}''$, $\frac{7}{32}''$, $\frac{1}{4}''$, and $\frac{5}{16}''$. Round the sides, leaving the bottom flat. The rounded sides are used to rub down cover material on the boards, the flat sides for rubbing down between the bands, and the grooves are to fit over the bands being worked.

PUTTING ON THE LEATHER BACK. Have everything ready before you start: waste newspaper cut into half sheets, paste, paste brush, bone folders, band sticks, and band nippers or a pair of flat-jaw, wide-nose pliers, such as glass-breaking pliers. If the jaws have serrated faces, cover them with a piece of masking tape to protect the leather.

Stand the book on its fore edge, or let it stand, loosely held between the jaws of a bench press (Illus. 168). Brush paste on the back of the book and work it in around the bands. Center the pasted leather over the back, stretch it down the sides and adhere it to the boards by rubbing with your fingers. Rub the leather down between the bands with a bone folder. As the excess leather creeps over the edges of the back, move it down the boards and over their edges by gentle rubbing.

Take the book out of the press and stand it on its spine, letting the boards drop open. Turn in the leather at the head so that the outer surface of the hollow back is between the leather of the back and the turn-in. Push the leather under the headband with a folder or a table knife. Rub it down along the edges of the boards and inside. Turn the book around and treat the tail end the same way. Close the boards on waxed paper to protect the book from the moisture in the paste.

THE HEADCAP. Sometimes, instead of headband and tailband, the book is provided with a headcap and a tailcap, the generic term headcap generally sufficing for both. To make a headcap, cut a length of cord the precise width of the back as measured over the curve. When you go to turn in the leather at head and tail,

lay a length of cord on the pasted side of the leather, just above the folds of the sections. Turn the leather in over the cord and under the back of the book. Adjust the cord so that it lies like a headband on the cut edge of the section folds, and rub down the leather above it so that it is flat, the cord standing out like a band in reverse and covering the section folds.

RUBBING UP THE BACK. Set the book up between grooving boards with the metals in the French grooves. The metals may be brass or aluminum, but steel will stain the leather. It is a good idea in any case, however, to put waxed paper between the book and the grooving boards to avoid accidental abrasion of the leather. Grip the arrangement by the fore edge in a bench press (Illus. 168) with just enough pressure to hold it firm.

Now select a band stick with a groove most closely approaching the width of the bands and carefully rub up each band with the band stick inside the groove as shown in the photo (Illus. 169). Do not apply too much pressure nor rub too hard. Treat all the bands until they stand out prominently. Rub down between the bands with the flat side of the stick.

BAND NIPPERS. (Illus. 170). Next squeeze the bands lightly with band nippers to adhere the leather to their sides and to straighten them up if they should be crooked. Band nippers are becoming more "old-fashioned" every day and exceedingly difficult, if not impossible, to obtain. A pair of wide-jawed glass-breaking pliers work quite well.

Leave the book now, but, for the next few hours, return to it from time to time and rub up the bands again and apply the nippers where necessary.

Lacking band sticks and nippers, you can approximate their service by using two wooden rulers with a square edge. Grip the band between them in rubbing up.

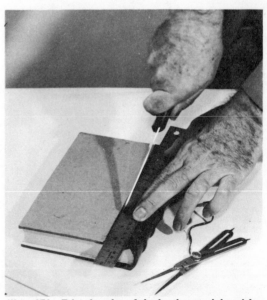

Illus. 171—Trim the edge of the leather straight with a beveled cut by tilting knife blade toward the back of the book.

Illus. 172—Bring the back edge of the siding up to the blinded-in line on the leather and rub it down with a folder or band stick.

TRIMMING THE SIDES. The next day, you can trim off the excess leather on the sides (Illus. 171). With dividers, mark the leather at the width of the line you originally drew, at both head and tail. Lay a straightedge along the marks and blind in a crease in the leather with

Illus. 173—Pinch up the corners of the turn-in and snip them off with scissors about $\frac{1}{4}$ inch above the board. Rub down the overlap.

94

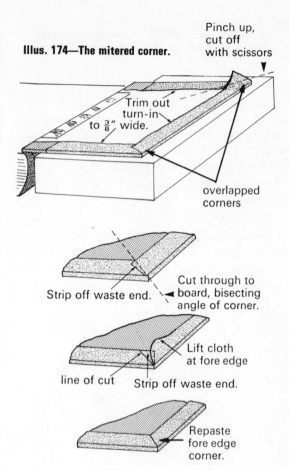

Illus. 174—The mitered corner.

Pinch up, cut off with scissors

Trim out turn-in to $\frac{3}{8}$" wide.

overlapped corners

Strip off waste end.

Cut through to board, bisecting angle of corner.

Lift cloth at fore edge

line of cut

Strip off waste end.

Repaste fore edge corner.

the rounded end of a bone folder. Run this line from head to tail on both sides of the book. Then take a straightedge and a knife and make a bevelled cut along the crease by tilting the knife blade toward the back of the book. Carry the cut over the edges at head and tail and in the width of the turn-in. Strip off the excess leather and rub down the leather edge with the folder.

SIDING. Cut the siding from whatever material is desired (red buckram shown; it goes well with red morocco). Allow for a $\frac{3}{4}$-inch turn-in at head, tail and fore edge.

Paste up the siding with the same paste used on the leather back, fold it over on itself and let it soak for 5 minutes. Paste again and let soak folded, then, after another 5 minutes, give it a third pasting. Smooth out the paste with your fingers, removing the lumps, if any. Bring the back edge of the pasted siding up to and over the crease at the edge of the leather (Illus. 172) and rub it down, first with your hand, then with a folder or a band stick. Squeeze the cover out in all directions, pulling the excess over the edges of the board. Rub down the edges, then open the board and turn the siding in at head and tail, then along the fore edge, and rub down.

THE MITERED CORNER. (Illus. 173). Pinch the corners of the buckram together and snip off with shears about a quarter of an inch above the board. Rub down, one edge overlapping the other. Miter when dry as shown in the diagram (Illus. 174).

PRESSING. (Illus. 175). Apply pressure to the siding only. Never press the leather or you will crush it and spoil its appearance.

THE HALF BINDING. (Illus. 176–178). The diagrams show how to mark the boards for the leather back and corners. The corners are pared all around and pasted on. When dry, put on the back. When the back is dry, trim all three inboard edges straight. Lay on a sheet of tracing paper and mark it so that it can be cut out to make a template for use in cutting the cover material.

For pressing the siding, make a pair of cardboard forms that will just cover the siding, leaving back and corners free.

Illus. 175—Set pressing boards on each side of book, even with back edge of siding. Apply pressure only to the siding. Slip sheet aluminum and waxed paper between boards and book.

Where the cover is to provide a fore edge trim instead of corners, first paste down the siding, then paste down the trim, overlapping the siding, and turn it in over the fore edge and around the corners.

COMPLETING THE BOOK. When the cover material is dry, open the boards and trim out the turn-in to $\frac{3}{8}$ inch wide. If water-base paste was used on the outer sides of the boards, a fill-in will be needed on the inner sides. Cut a piece of newsprint or newspaper for each board and paste it to the inner side. Close the boards

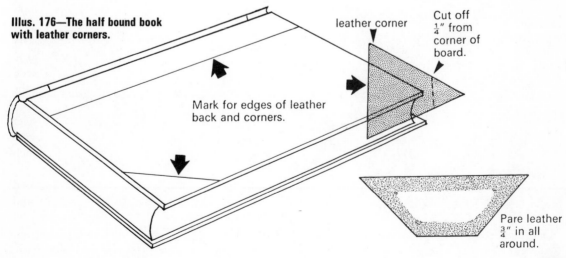

Illus. 176—The half bound book with leather corners.

leather corner

Cut off $\frac{1}{4}$" from corner of board.

Mark for edges of leather back and corners.

Pare leather $\frac{3}{4}$" in all around.

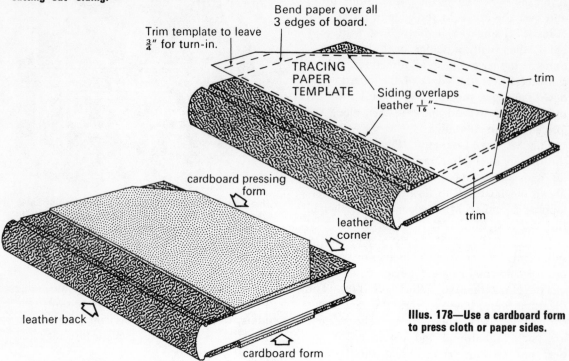

Illus. 177—Make a paper template for cutting out siding.

Trim template to leave ¾" for turn-in.

Bend paper over all 3 edges of board.

TRACING PAPER TEMPLATE

Siding overlaps leather $\frac{1}{16}$":

trim

trim

cardboard pressing form

leather corner

leather back

cardboard form

Illus. 178—Use a cardboard form to press cloth or paper sides.

on waxed paper and press overnight, then paste down the board paper and leave in the press until dry. If non-warping paste was used outside, omit the fill and paste down the board paper with non-warping paste.

12. Flexible Sewing

Why this type of sewing is called "flexible" is a mystery, since the leather cover is pasted directly to the back, making it less flexible than a book with a hollow back. At any rate, it is undoubtedly the earliest type of sewing invented for bookbinding. A better term would be "sewing on exterior cords," since the cords lie outside the folds of the sections instead of being buried within them.

In the earliest books, the cords were of leather or some similar material and they were attached to wooden boards fitted with catches and even keyed locks on the fore edge to hold the book shut against the expansive energy of parchment leaves.

THE CORDS. There are three ways to string the sewing table. In all cases, at least 5 cords are used, and in one way of sewing, the kettle stitches are buried in sawcuts at head and tail, the sewing cords all being single. In the second way, 5 sets of *double* cords are strung; that is, two cords at each cord position; and the kettle stitches are buried in saw cuts. In the third method, the back is not sawed at all. Five sets of double cords are strung, and a single cord is strung at the head and another at the tail, around which the kettle stitches are made.

Forwarding the book up to the point where it is ready for sewing is carried out as described in previous chapters. While the repaired sections are pressing, get the endpapers ready, for these are to be sewed into the book.

CLOTH-JOINT ENDPAPERS. (Illus. 180). Since flexible sewing puts extra strain on the hinges every time the boards are opened, and since no backing cloth is used to strengthen the hinge, the endpapers have to be provided with a cloth joint.

The illustration shows the sheets needed for one set of endpapers. The sheets A and B, indicated as "colored," can be colored paper, paper that has been printed with a design, pastel paper, or plain white paper which you

Illus. 179—A comparison of styles. (Left) Quarter bound in red morocco, light red buckram sides, French groove. Flour-and-water paste used throughout. (Right) Flexible sewing with laced boards. Quarter bound in medium tan morocco, dark red siding. Non-warping paste used throughout.

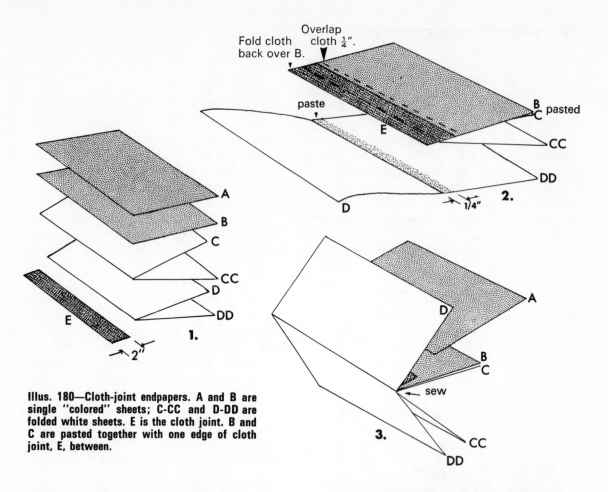

Illus. 180—Cloth-joint endpapers. A and B are single "colored" sheets; C-CC and D-DD are folded white sheets. E is the cloth joint. B and C are pasted together with one edge of cloth joint, E, between.

have colored yourself by dipping it into a bath of acrylic tube paint diluted with water.

The cloth hinge may be unbleached muslin or cotton canvas, book cloth, artificial leather, etc. Plain cloth should be starched first and ironed dry. Ready-made starch in a spray can is very good for odd jobs like this.

Cut all the sheets of paper oversize—that is, larger than the book. When the endpapers have been folded, pasted and are ready for sewing, trim them to the size of the book with a straightedge and a knife.

In pasting up the joint-sheets, brush paste on C, then rub the cloth joint down along the fold and ¾ inch in. This will leave a half inch of the cloth exposed when sheet B is rubbed down on C so as to overlap the cloth ¼ inch. Put waxed paper on each side of the pasted

sheets and put between plain pressing boards. Press under heavy pressure until the next day.

Colored sheet A does not have to be cut until you are ready for it, as it will be the board paper. CC of the pasted sheets is to be pasted down to leaf DD as indicated at 2. Illus. 180–3 shows the assembled endpapers, ready for sewing to the book. Mark the outside sheet "Waste Leaf"—it will be torn out and discarded when the board papers are pasted down.

MARKING THE BACK. (Illus. 181A). Spacing the cords for flexible sewing is different in that three of the included spaces are equal in size while the fourth, at the head, may be either larger or smaller, as needed to contain the title of the book. Note too that the space at the head, above the topmost cord, is shorter than the equivalent space at the tail. This gives the back

98

a better optical balance when viewed on the shelf. Make the marks across the back with a fine-point, felt-tip marker and be sure to mark the fold of every section. Saw in only the head and tail kettle-stitch marks.

SEWING ON EXTERIOR CORDS. The example is being sewed on single cords (Illus. 181B, 182). Note how the sewing thread is wrapped around the cord. This means you must pull up each stitch as it is made, as you cannot "pull through" a thread wrapped around 5 cords. As in tape sewing, puncture each section at the cord marks. A needle gripped in a small pin vice (Illus. 182) gives better control, and a saddle such as the one in Illus. 154 ensures accuracy in locating the puncture.

Sew all-along and off-and-on as usual and tie off the thread with a couple of kettle stitches. In cutting off the thread, leave an inch or so to be pasted down to the back.

Release the tension on the cords and cut them off several inches long on either side of the book. You cannot pull the cords through as you can when sewing on buried cords.

ROUNDING AND BACKING. The flexibly sewed book has to be rounded, backed *and boarded* before it is trimmed. Trimming in this manner is called "trimming in boards."

Since the book will have tight joints, the turn-up of the backing groove must be equal to the thickness of the board. Mark the waste sheets for backing with this in mind.

Take care in backing to avoid a heavy blow on a cord, which might mash it or even cut a stitch or two. When the book has been backed, leave it between the backing boards, brush the back liberally with paste, then scrape off all the old glue, but do not reglue. To ensure that the back will hold its shape throughout subsequent forwarding operations, leave the book in press until the back is thoroughly dry.

THE BOARDS. If the book is to be trimmed on all three edges (head, tail and fore edge), cut the boards to the exact measure of the waste leaf, from head to tail and from backing groove to fore edge.

A clean, deckle-edged fore edge (Illus. 196) may not require trimming. In this case, the

Illus. 181—Flexible sewing on exterior cords.

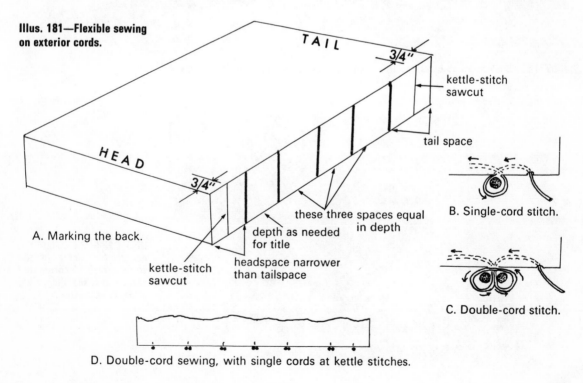

A. Marking the back.

B. Single-cord stitch.

C. Double-cord stitch.

D. Double-cord sewing, with single cords at kettle stitches.

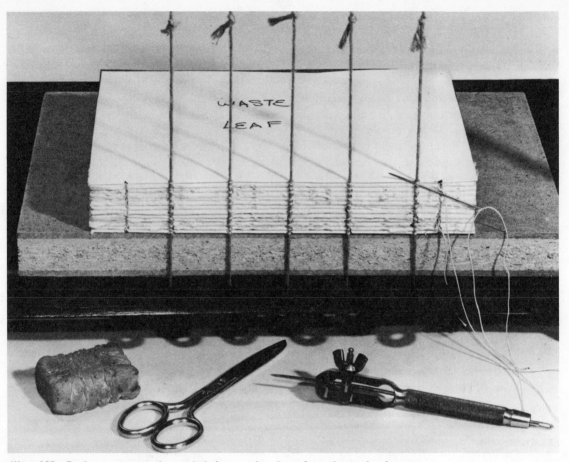

Illus. 182—Book sewn on exterior cords before cutting down from the sewing frame.

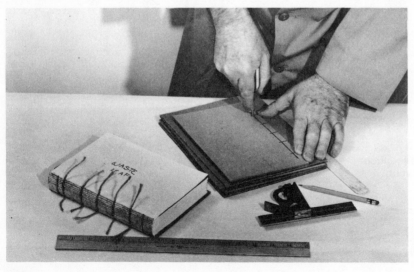

Illus. 183—Punching the boards for lacing in the cords. Stack of corrugated cardbord takes the point, protects table top.

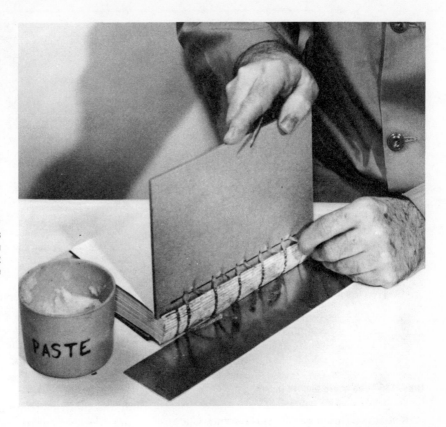

square should be accounted for in the width of the boards by adding $\frac{1}{8}$ inch.

Sometimes only the head may be trimmed, and in this case, account for the square at both fore edge and tail by adding $\frac{1}{8}$ inch to both measures. Another time, the head and fore edge may be trimmed, while the tail is deckle-edged; thus, the measure of the tail square only is added to the height of the boards.

As you can see, there is no general rule to be applied to all books. Each book must be treated as the individual it is.

LACING ON THE BOARDS. On the outer face of each board, rule a pencil line from head to tail, $\frac{3}{8}$ inch from the back edge (for an 8vo size, less for a smaller book, more for a larger) (Illus. 185A). Rule a similar line on the inside of each board, a little farther in.

Adjust the boards on the book and mark the back edge of each where each cord comes. Use a square to carry the marks over to the ruled line. Punch through each mark with an awl (Illus. 183) and enlarge the hole for easy passage of the cord. Cut a triangular-shaped channel, half way through the board, from each hole to the back edge (Illus. 185A). The cords will lie in these channels and will not easily betray their presence through the leather cover.

Turn the board over and mark the second series of holes on the ruled line, each hole about $\frac{3}{8}$ inch below (toward the tail) its companion hole. Punch these holes through from the inner face of the board. Do not flatten or trim off the lump around the exit side of each hole.

Fray out the cords against a piece of sheet metal and reduce their bulk toward the ends by scraping with a knife. Twist the tips to a point with a little paste between your fingers. Stand the board on edge in the backing groove and feed the cords through from the outside, then back out through the second set of holes (Illus. 184, 185B).

Turn the book over and lace in the end board the same way.

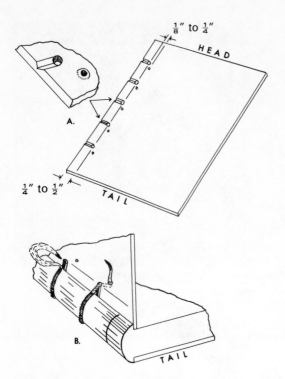

Illus. 186—Knocking down the lacing. Light hammering closes the holes on the cords, securing them.

Illus. 185—The board and its lacing.

KNOCKING DOWN THE BOARD LACING. Clamp the knocking-down block (or iron) in the end of the lying press. Rub paste into the holes in both boards and over the cords *inside* the board. Do not paste the cords in the grooves on the outside until ready to cover, as the boards must have complete freedom of movement for trimming.

Hold the book with the board flat on the block (Illus. 186) and gently hammer the holes shut around the cords; first the secondary set of holes from the outside. Then turn the board over and knock down the holes nearest the back edge.

Close the boards on waxed paper and trim off the projecting ends of cords with a razor blade (Illus. 187). Adjust the boards square with the book, place waxed paper on the outside and sandwich between plain pressing boards. Press under heavy pressure until the following day.

TRIMMING IN BOARDS. When trimming in boards, trim the head first, then the tail, and finally, the fore edge. Open the front board and mark a trim line across the top edge of the waste sheet, $\frac{1}{8}$ inch down from the top edge and at right angles to the backing groove. Use a square to ensure this.

Slip a piece of thin cardboard between the end board and the book to take the knife point at the finish of trimming. Cutting boards are not used when trimming in boards, as the attached boards serve the same purpose. Pull the front board down until its upper edge is even with the line drawn across the waste leaf (Illus. 188A).

The minimum amount of trim should be $\frac{1}{8}$

Illus. 187—After lacing, trim off the protruding ends of the cords with a razor blade.

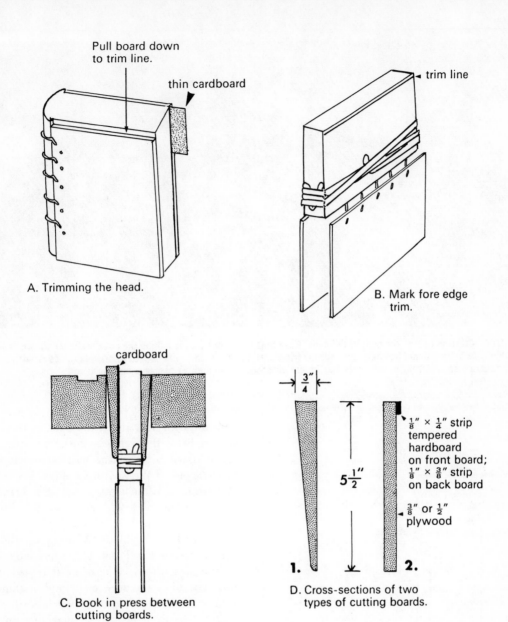

Pull board down
to trim line.

thin cardboard

A. Trimming the head.

trim line

B. Mark fore edge
   trim.

cardboard

C. Book in press between
   cutting boards.

$5\frac{1}{2}''$

$\frac{3}{4}''$

1.

2.

$\frac{1}{8}'' \times \frac{1}{4}''$ strip
tempered
hardboard
on front board;
$\frac{1}{8}'' \times \frac{3}{8}''$ strip
on back board

$\frac{3}{8}''$ or $\frac{1}{2}''$
plywood

D. Cross-sections of two
   types of cutting boards.

Illus. 188—Trimming in boards.

inch, which will provide the book with squares $\frac{1}{8}$ inch wide. Sometimes, however, it may prove necessary to increase the size of the square, when a wider overhang of the boards is desired to accommodate oversize headbands or for some other reason. Where this is so, it may not be possible to pull the board down far enough

to meet the trim line without distorting the book.

In this case, cut a secondary board the same size as the attached board. Swing the attached board wide open and back out of the way behind the book and place the secondary board up against the backing groove and even

103

Illus. 189—Starting to trim the head of the book. Note that the front board is behind the book, between the press bars, and that a secondary board has been used for the front cutting board. This was needed to provide the book with extra-large squares, so the front board could not be pulled down far enough to act as a cutting board.

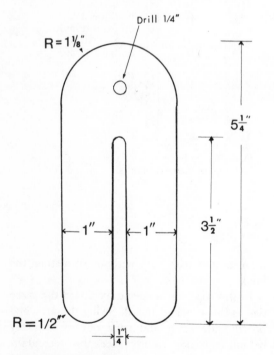

Illus. 190—The trindle.

with the trim line. Insert the book in the press and tighten the screws. Push the attached board down between the bars of the press so as to be out of the way of the plow knife, and proceed to trim the head (Illus. 189). Trim the tail the same way. In both cases, finish by trimming off the turn-up of the far backing groove with a long-bladed knife (Illus. 124).

FLATTENING THE BACK. If the fore edge is to be trimmed, the back must be flattened, thus also flattening the fore edge and making it square across so that it may be trimmed.

Open the front board and mark a trim line $\frac{1}{8}$ inch from the fore edge (Illus. 188B). Measure to make sure that the trim line is equidistant from the backing groove at both head and tail.

Horseshoe-shaped "trindles" (Illus. 190, 191, 192) are used to flatten the back. You can make your own trindles, from wood or metal as indicated in the photos. Dimensions given in Illus. 190 are suitable for most books; very small or very large books might require these to be reduced or enlarged. In a pinch, you could

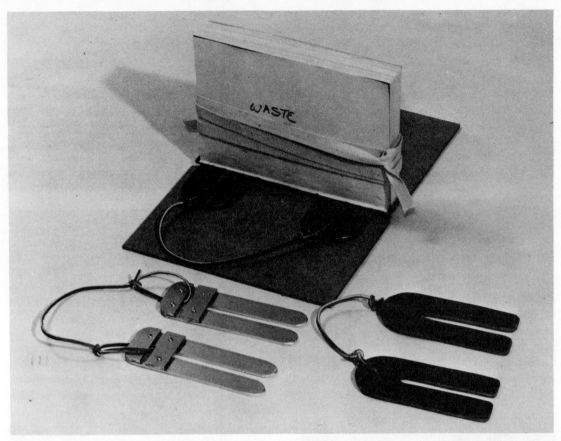

Illus. 191—The back of the book has been lifted and flattened with a pair of $\frac{3}{32}$"-thick steel trindles. At right is a pair of trindles made of $\frac{1}{8}$" tempered hardboard. They can also be made of hardwood. At left is a pair fabricated by glueing and pop-riveting pieces of strip aluminum together, $\frac{1}{8}$" × $\frac{3}{4}$".

substitute a pair of aluminum or plated steel strips, a couple of rulers or table knives.

Hold the book by the body and let both boards drop down. Slip a trindle astride the cord at the head at a downward angle. Insert the second trindle around the cord closest to the tail. (Since the trindles are always used in pairs, secure them to one another with a length of cord or leather thong.)

Press down on the rounded end of the trindle at the head, levering it against the back edge of the board, thus lifting the ends of the legs so that they may be passed through between the book and the other board, thus lifting and flattening the back. Do the same with the trindle at the tail. Set the book flat on the table (Illus. 191) and proceed to wrap it with 3 or 4 turns of twill tape. Secure the tape by tucking the end in under the turns. Now remove the trindles; the tape will hold the book in shape for adjusting in the trimming press.

CUTTING BOARDS. The tape wrapped around the book will mark it if flat cutting boards are used, so that the pressure of the press is distributed evenly over them. Illus. 188D shows cross-sections of two types of cutting boards. #1 is made from a length of hardwood 1′×6′, the outer face bevelled, either on a jointer-planer, or using a planer accessory on a radial arm saw. The other board, #2, is a piece of ⅜-inch or ½-inch-thick plywood with a

Illus. 192—You can make your own trindles out of hardwood $\frac{1}{8}$ inch thick, hardboard, aluminum, or $\frac{3}{32}$ inch steel, using a jig saw. Round all corners and edges to prevent scoring the book.

strip of hardboard glued along the upper edge, in the same way the backing boards were treated and explained in a previous chapter. A pair of either type, about 12 inches long, will localize the press pressure along the trim line, allowing the bottom edges of the boards to swing slightly apart, thus avoiding what might be a cutting pressure on the book along those same edges.

TRIMMING THE FORE EDGE. Place a piece of cardboard between the back cutting board and the book to take the plow point at the finish of cutting and insert the book and cutting boards into the lying press as diagrammed in Illus. 188C. Check the book for squareness and tighten the press as usual, then go ahead and trim the fore edge with the plow.

NICKING THE BOARDS. Nick the back corners of both boards (Illus. 78, Chapter 7) after the book has been trimmed.

HANDMADE HEADBANDS. A fine leather binding should have something special in the way of headbands, though you can use the commercial kind, as previously described.

In olden times, headbands were created with colored silk threads, actually sewed to the book. Every third or fourth section, the needle was passed through the fold to tie the headband down.

Handsome though the result of such sewing might be, the procedure is fraught with danger for the beginner, as it is very easy to damage the cut head of the book and produce an unsightly appearance to offset the gain of the headband.

Sewed headbands can be created off the book, however, using your own choice of two

Illus. 193—Headband gripped in a vice leaves both hands free to wield the needles. The small, plastic, spring clothespin holds the cord in position until a few stitches have been made, then it is removed. The cord may also be stuck to the muslin backing with paste. Yellow and blue silk embroidery threads are used here.

or more colors of silk twist or rayon embroidery thread. Compared to the commercial variety, such headbands sparkle with color.

The basis of the headband is a strip of unbleached muslin, sprayed with or dipped into starch and ironed dry to stiffen it and make it more manageable. Cut the length of the strip parallel to the selvedge of the cloth. Its width should be about a half inch wider than the width of the back of the book. Cut the strip in two and turn over one short edge of each piece about ⅛ inch, and iron it down. This provides a top edge that will not fray. To start with, each piece of muslin should be longer than the tail space, so that the headbands can be trimmed to exact size later on.

You will find the work easier and faster to accomplish if you grip the muslin, creased edge up, in a small vice (Illus. 193), thus leaving both hands free for the work. Cut a length of sewing cord or thin leather strip as long as the width of the muslin and either pinch it to the cloth, as in Illus. 193, or paste it along the creased edge of cloth and wait for the paste to dry.

Step 1. Take two thin needles with large, oval eyes and thread one with yellow silk twist or nylon embroidery thread. Thread the other with blue thread. Each thread is about 30 inches long to ensure having enough to sew the entire headband without adding on. *Step 2.* Take the needle with yellow thread and nip it under a few threads at the back of the muslin at position X in Illus. 194A. Pull the thread through, except for about 2 inches at the end. *Step 3.* Make 2 to 4 whipstitches around the cord, from back to front. Pull up the stitches and press them together so that no spaces show between the threads. *Step 4.* Take the blue thread and pass the needle directly through the muslin, under the cord, at position X, bringing it out on the left side of the series of yellow stitches (Illus. 194B). Bring the blue thread across under the yellow stitches, and pass the needle back through the muslin, under the cord, at the right of the yellow series, so that it can start a series of blue stitches from the

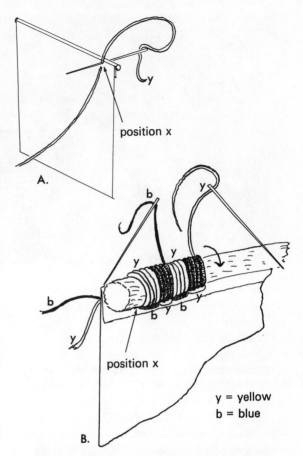

Illus. 194—Whipstitching the handmade headband.

back of the headband. *Step 5.* Make the same number of blue whipstitches around the cord as you did with the yellow, and leave the needle behind the work. *Step 6.* Take up the yellow again and pass the needle through from back to front, under the cord, where the series of blue whipstitches begins. Carry the yellow across under the blue stitches and back through the muslin under the cord. *Step 7.* Continue with the yellow thread and make the same number of whipstitches once more around the cord and leave the needle behind. Continue in this manner, alternating colors, until the headband has been whipstitched long enough to cross the back of the book. Study of the diagram in Illus. 194B will make the procedure clear. *Step 8.* When the sewing has been completed,

107

Illus. 195—Light kraft paper glued over the headbands is being rubbed down with a folder.

tie the ends of the yellow and blue threads together at both ends of the headband and cut the threads off short. Smear a little Elmer's Glue-All on both knots to keep them from slipping apart.

HEADBANDING THE BOOK. When you have sewed both headbands, trim off the excess muslin on both sides, leaving only the width of the back of the book. Use a knife and straightedge. Next, trim the length of one muslin to fit the space from the head of the book to the first cord; trim the length of the other to fit the tail space, from the last cord to the tail of the book.

If you are making such headbands as these for a book sewed on buried cords, trim off the muslin to reach only as far as the line of kettlestitches at both head and tail, as the super or backing cloth compensates for the space in between them.

Glue the muslin down to the back of the book with the cord overhanging the folds of the sections. Allow the glue to set for a bit, then glue down over both pieces of muslin a piece of thin kraft paper, reaching from the outermost edge of the headband to the band or sewing cord. Rub down thoroughly with a bone folder (Illus. 195). Illus. 196 shows how

the handmade headband looks on the finished book (note the deckled fore edge, which was not trimmed).

BUILDING UP THE BANDS. If you want only small bands showing on the back of the book, you can go ahead and cover without further

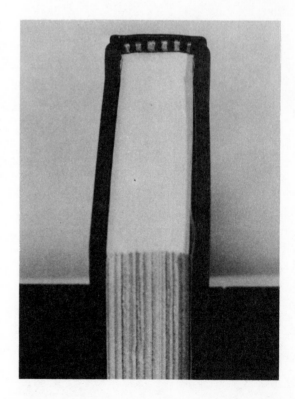

Illus. 196—The handmade, sewed-silk headband of yellow and blue embroidery thread on the finished book.

Illus. 197—This is how the cords of this book were built up by glueing a piece of cord alongside each sewn cord and covering both with a strip of leather. Trim the overhang off on both sides after the glue has dried, but take care not to cut through the laced cords.

treatment. However, the bands can be built up so as to provide a more imposing appearance. In the example (Illus. 197), a minimum of build-up is provided to show how it is done. The photo and caption are self-explanatory.

Where sewing has been done on double cords, you can apply the leather superstructure directly to both cords without further widening.

COVERING. The flexibly sewn book may be given a quarter, half or full binding in leather. Before covering, nick the back corners of the boards as shown in Illus. 78 and 80, Chapter 7.

Illus. 198 shows how to use a block plane to thin the pared leather back for a quarter binding. Apply the leather to the back the same way it was done in Chapter 11, over false bands. This time, however, while the leather is soaking up paste, brush paste also on the back and work it in well around the bands. As in that instance, too, you can use either non-warping paste or flour-and-water paste, the latter being rather easier to work with as it has greater wetting power.

FULL LEATHER BINDING. Measure the book for its cover by wrapping a strip of paper around and creasing it over the fore edges of the boards. Cut the leather to allow for a full inch of turn-in all around. Pare the edges an inch in, using the paring knife or the bull-nose rabbet plane. Also pare a little thinness into the region of the hinges. If the back is too thick for easy stretching over the bands, thin it down with the block plane (Illus. 198) or the spokeshave (Illus. 167, Chapter 11). It is not necessary to thin the leather covering the sides.

Lay out the pasted leather (that has been allowed to soak 5 or 10 minutes) on the table and position the book at one end. Brush paste on the back of the book and into the cordgrooves on the boards. Lift the far end of the leather and bring it forward over the book. Stretch it tight against the back, then lay it down on the board.

Stand the book on its fore edge and rub down between the bands with a folder. Rub the leather downwards on both sides with your

109

Illus. 198—A block plane can be used to thin the leather back on a slab of glass. The extra-small (3½″) block plane (left foreground) has a blade 1″ wide and is useful for local thinning over small areas.

hands, smoothing it out over the boards. If it wrinkles, lift it free, then replace it carefully and rub down as before, rubbing from the back toward all three edges of the boards.

Either pinch up the corners and cut them off with scissors for a mitered corner, or cut the corners off at a 45° angle, ¼ inch from each board corner, before turning in the leather. Work the leather over the edges, rubbing down to ensure good adhesion, and move the excess on down into the turn-in.

Place a piece of flashing aluminum between each board and the book to ensure adhesion of the leather to the squares. Place waxed paper between board and aluminum to keep the latter free of paste.

Sandwich the book between plain pressing boards and put aside with a brick on top to weight it down. Leave overnight (Illus. 199).

OPENING THE BOARDS. When the book is thoroughly dry, the joints are stiff and, if you open the boards hastily, you run the risk of tearing the leather loose along the back edge.

Therefore, always open a flexibly-sewn book in this special way: take the fore edge of the front board in your right hand, at the same time pressing with the edge of your left palm along the back edge of the board. Keep in mind that the *hinge* of the joint is the leather cover at the *top* of the backing groove. When the board is opened wide, its back edge must be even with the top edge of the backing groove turn-up.

Now carefully raise the fore edge and, at the same time, push the board back toward the backing groove, holding the back edge in place with your left hand. Slowly bring the board over, maintaining the position of the joint with your left hand, until it is opened wide. Now work the joint a few times to loosen it; then turn the book over and open the end board the same way.

FILLING IN THE BOARDS. The first step is to trim out the turn-in to ⅜ inch wide, using a knife and a straightedge. The cut edge of the leather will be quite thick—and even an edge of buckram will have some thickness. To make

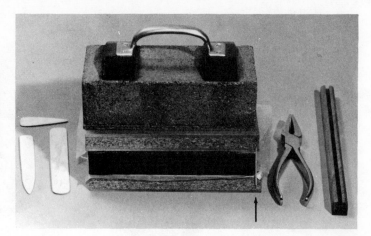

Illus. 199—After the leather has been well rubbed down and the bands pinched straight and even, place the book between pressing boards with a brick on top. Use a piece of sewing thread to tie up the joints. Here a toothpick was twisted in the loop of thread to take up the slack and tighten it. Note toothpick at head of book (right).

the inside of the board flat, this hollow will have to be filled with a piece of paper or thin cardboard cut to the precise dimensions of the space bordered by the trimmed turn-in. Such a sheet is called a "fill-in," or "fill sheet" (Illus. 200).

A single sheet of newsprint is sufficient fill for a half or quarter binding sided with buckram or a moderately thick paper.

Since the purpose of the fill is only to take up space and not to counteract the pull of the pasted leather on the outside, glue the sheet in with hot, hard glue, Elmer's Glue-All, or non-warping paste. Close the boards on waxed paper and press in the screw or standing press overnight.

The board lining (Illus. 200–1) is used *only* if flour-and-water paste (formula on page 157)

Illus. 200—Order of treatment of inside of board.

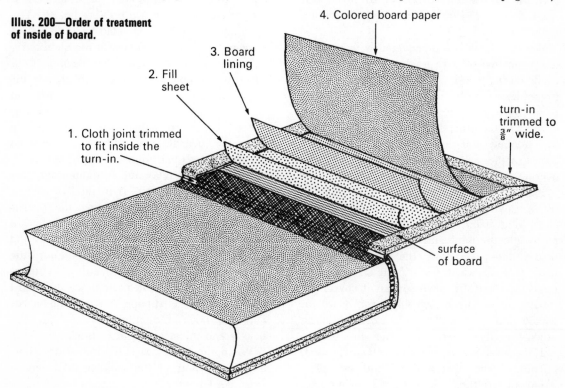

4. Colored board paper

3. Board lining

2. Fill sheet

1. Cloth joint trimmed to fit inside the turn-in.

turn-in trimmed to $\frac{3}{8}$" wide.

surface of board

Illus. 201—The book pasted down open. Note the E-shaped cardboard support holding the boards in position. Make the center bar of the E as wide as the back of the book. Although dry, the boards show no indication of warping, owing to the fact that non-warping paste was used on both sides of the boards.

was used to paste down the cover. If non-warping paste was used outside the boards, it must also be used inside, and the board lining may be omitted.

Where a book is fully covered with leather, it is often tooled with gold both outside and inside on the turn-in. Whether or not you wish to tool inside the board, you can cut the board paper to fit precisely inside the turn-in of the cover. On the other hand, if there is to be no such tooling, you may instead cut the board paper to the same size as the flyleaf, so as to overlap the turn-in.

PASTING DOWN OPEN. First, tear out the waste leaves and discard them. Then trim the cloth joint as indicated in Illus. 200–1, brush paste into the joint and over the edge of the board, and paste down the cloth joint. Immediately afterward, brush paste on the board paper and paste it down so that it covers the cloth joint on the board. Close the board on waxed paper, turn the book over, and paste down the other board paper the same way.

If the book were to dry with its boards closed, opening the boards would tear the endpapers. To avoid this, the book is "pasted down open"

(Illus. 201). That is, both boards are opened and extended behind the book, which is supported on one or two pressing boards. The open boards are held extended by an E-shaped piece of cardboard as shown in the photo.

If flour-and-water paste has been used in covering and board papering the book, a result of pasting down open is that the boards will warp as they dry. This is no problem, however. When the board papers are dry, carefully close the boards, place the book between pressing boards and under a weight and leave until the boards relax and straighten out.

PASTING DOWN SHUT. A method of pasting down shut that avoids warping the boards (when flour-and-water paste is used), is first to paste down only the cloth joints and leave the book in the paste-down-open position until the paste dries. Then work the boards a few times to limber the joints and paste down the board papers. Place waxed paper between the boards and the book and press between pressing boards and under a weight (a brick).

When the book has had time to dry thoroughly, open it in the manner indicated in Illus. 98, Chapter 7.

13. Single-Sheet Binding

Binding typewritten material, such as theses, reports, manuscripts, the annual aggregation of club minutes, or other typewritten, mimeographed, or printed material consisting of single sheets, requires special methods of handling. In this chapter, we shall consider some of the treatments for these and other sources of single-sheet material.

MACHINE STITCHING. A stapling machine may be used in bindery operations. Disregard-

ing those in professional use, there are a number of relatively inexpensive machines made for use in the home or office which suit the amateur's purposes. (See Sources of Supply in Appendix.)

Folded pamphlets, typewritten or mimeographed, containing stories, poems, club news, or similar material, can be saddle stitched; *i.e.*, stapled through the fold, the staples being clinched on the inside (Illus. 202–204). Lacking

Illus. 202—Examples of single-sheet binding demonstrated in this chapter. The paper-covered books in foreground are stapled; first book on left is side-stitched with the sewing awl; then four issues of National Geographic magazine bound with whipstitch sewing; the last three are perfect bound, and the last book is backed.

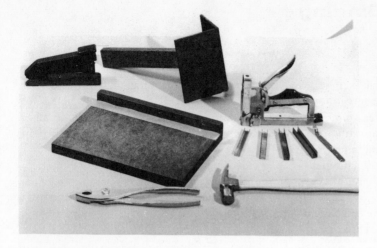

a saddle-stitching stapler, you can make a saddle like the one in Illus. 203, which is open along the ridge to let the staples through. The desk stapler can be opened out and used as a tacker to drive staples through the fold; then you can bend those over inside with a staple extractor, spoon, or similar implement. Also on the market is a long-reach stapler permitting you to staple through a fold as far as 12 inches from the fore edge. Like the Swingline Saddle Stitcher, this one also clinches its own staples.

Manuscripts up to about $\frac{3}{8}$ inch thick can be side stitched with a heavy duty stapler designed to staple as many as 100 or more sheets of paper (Illus. 206). Also, the staple driver, or staple gun, can be adapted to bindery use as shown in Illus. 207. Staples are available for such machines from $\frac{1}{4}$ to $\frac{9}{16}$ inch long. A staple about $\frac{1}{8}$ inch longer than the thickness of the work should be chosen. As the device shown is non-clinching, the staples must be bent over by hand and tapped with a hammer to imbed them. Do not use this type of stapler for saddle stitching as described above, as the staples are too heavy for such use.

PREPARING THE BOOK FOR STITCHING. When preparing single sheets for side stitching, first cut two sheets of white endpaper stock or heavy drawing paper to the same size as the book and place a sheet on each side of the sheaf of paper. If the back edge has been damaged or mutilated (as often occurs with magazines that have been glued and side stitched), or if you wish to diminish the page size greatly, trim off the back edge with the guillotine or the press and plow. If the sheaf has been trimmed in a guillotine, grip it firmly and handle carefully to prevent slippage when transferring it to the glueing clamp for glueing. When trimmed with press and plow, glue up the back before removing the book from the lying press.

Most manuscripts on typing paper, however,

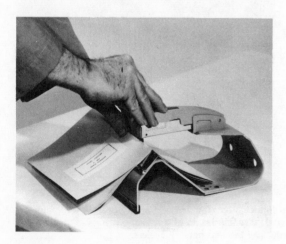

Illus. 204—The Swingline No. 615 Saddle Stapler staples booklets through the fold, and clinches the staples inside.

Illus. 205—The first step in binding single sheets is to trim the back with a guillotine or press and plow. A sheaf of typing paper, for example, needs only to have the back evened up with a Surform Shaver. Use it with short, quick strokes like a hen scratching feed. Do the final smoothing with a grit file (two types are shown in foreground), or with medium fine garnet paper wrapped around a wood block.

Illus. 206—The Bates H-30 heavy-duty stapler with Power Arm. It takes $\frac{1}{4}$-, $\frac{3}{8}$-, and $\frac{1}{2}$-inch staples and will side stitch up to 100 sheets of paper—more of thinner paper. The plywood table with hardboard top is home-made—not commercially available.

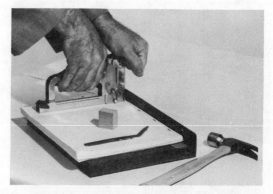

Illus. 207—Side stitching with the staple gun. The back guide automatically spaces the staples $\frac{1}{4}$ inch from the edge. The staples drive through into a corrugated card-board strip in back channel and are bent over by hand, then hammered down. The wood block is used against the bow of the staple to set it firmly into the paper after driving.

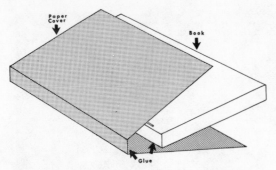

Illus. 208—A simple cover for the side-stitched book.

and, indeed, most magazines originally bound in single-sheet style, will not require the back to be trimmed. Instead, clamp the book in the glueing clamp, then grip the fore edge in the lying press with a piece of $\frac{1}{16}$-inch thick cardboard under each end of the clamp. Squeeze the lying press hand tight, remove the cardboards, then loosen the glueing clamp and let it drop on the cheeks of the press, exposing $\frac{1}{16}$ inch of the back edge of the single-sheet

sheaf. Plane the back edge down with a Surform Shaver (Illus. 205), which works faster than the more cumbersome plane. Finishing with a grit file or garnet paper (always wrap it around a block of wood) provides a smooth, even surface with the edge of every sheet exposed to the glue.

Before glueing, raise the clamp again to the level of the back and turn the screws up tight. Brush the back with Planatol BB, if available. This is a resinous glue made in West Germany especially for bindery use in binding single sheets (see Sources of Supply in Appendix). Effective for the purpose also is Elmer's Glue-All. Allow the back to dry—which should take about 15 to 20 minutes.

When side stitching with a stapler, drive

Illus. 209—The Dremel Moto-Tool provides a speedy way to drill manuscripts and similar single-sheet books for side stitching. The clamp is a piece of $1'' \times 1\frac{1}{4}'' \times \frac{1}{8}''$ aluminum angle, drilled with $\frac{3}{32}''$ holes, $\frac{3}{16}''$ from the edge, at half-inch intervals. Use the variable speed Moto Tool at half speed—No. 4 on the speed dial.

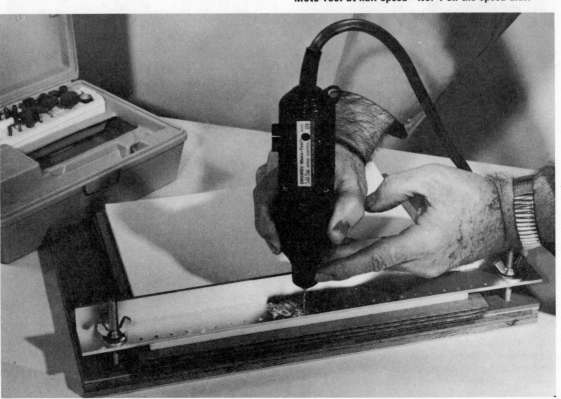

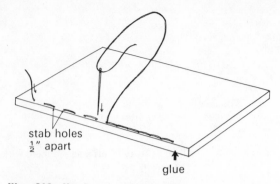

stab holes
½" apart

glue

Illus. 210—Hand-sewn side stitching.

the staples through from the front of the book (Illus. 206–207), $\frac{1}{8}$ to $\frac{1}{4}$ inch from the back edge, depending on the width of margin available in the gutter (the margin at the back edge of each page). Fold a cover from cover paper or Manila tag stock (Illus. 208) and glue the book into it. Rub the spine down thoroughly with a folder to be sure it sticks. When the glue has dried, trim the head, tail and fore edge.

When trimming with the guillotine, it is always a good idea to place a pad of cut-to-size newspaper under the book for the blade to enter after it has cut through the last sheet of the book, particularly if this is a sheet of heavy cover paper. Otherwise, if the cutting stick under the blade is well used, it will leave a ragged edge on the final sheet.

If you want to finish the book up nicely, you could cut a title and design in a linoleum or a wood block and print the cover paper before folding and glueing it to the book. The simplest way to finish such a book, however, is to hand letter or typewrite the title on a piece of paper and glue it to the front cover with Elmer's Glue-All. At the same time, type the entire title out in a straight line, cut out the narrow strip containing the title, and paste it to the spine of the book, reading from head to tail in the position shown in Illus. 202.

STABBING (DRILLING) FOR HAND STITCHING. Books such as those under discussion can also be side stitched by hand. There are two ways to do this. First, as when stapling, place a sheet of heavy white paper on either side of the sheaf, then plane and glue the back edge.

If the sheaf is very thin, you can rule a line

Illus. 211—The sewing awl creates a locked stitch at every stab hole. Wind the bobbin with No. 20 linen book thread.

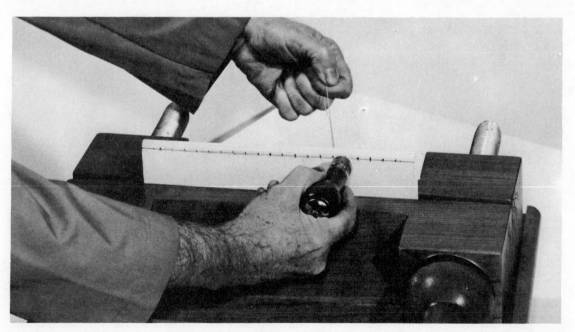

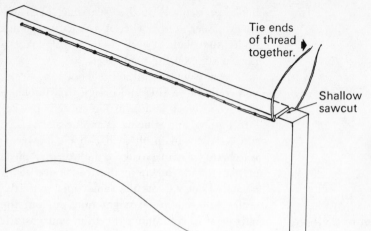

Tie ends
of thread
together.

Shallow
sawcut

Illus. 212—Tying off side stitching with the sewing awl.

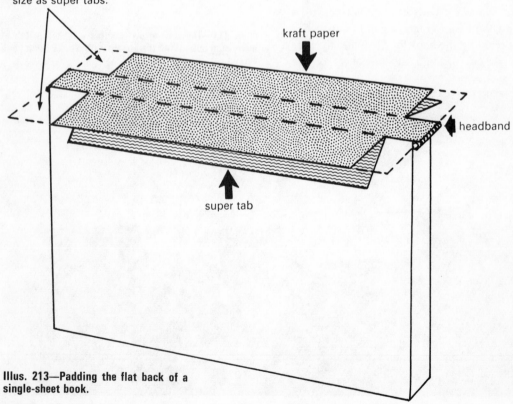

Cut off all 4
corners; make
paper tabs same
size as super tabs.

kraft paper

headband

super tab

Illus. 213—Padding the flat back of a single-sheet book.

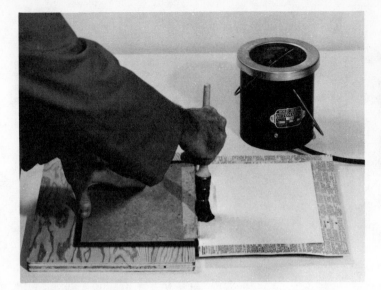

Illus. 214 — The awl-sewed book, boarded and covered with imitation leather. The same glue used to stick down the cover is repeated on the board paper. The automatic electric glue pot keeps constant, correct heat, does not use water so cannot run dry. If you buy one of these, buy an extra container for it—one for hard glue (marked H), the other for flexible glue (marked F).

down the back edge and make a mark every half inch for stab holes, leaving $\frac{3}{4}$ inch clear at head and tail. With a sharp-pointed awl, punch through the sheaf at each stab mark.

Thicker material, however, must be drilled. A stabbing clamp like the one shown in Illus. 209 is easy to make—or have made—and it will grip the book so as to keep the back from coming apart while drilling. The Dremel Moto-Tool speeds up the work considerably. Note several thicknesses of corrugated cardboard have been placed under the work to take the point of the drill. This protects the clamp table and the drill-point will stay sharp longer. Not too much pressure needs to be applied by the two $\frac{5}{16}$-inch carriage bolts with wing nuts.

A $\frac{1}{16}$-inch drill bit (shown) is used if you plan to sew with the sewing awl. Sewing by hand with a needle employs a thinner needle, so drill with an 18-gauge, $1\frac{1}{2}$-inch brad with the head cut off. The diamond point on the brad acts the same as a drill point. In either case, wax the drill bit on a cake of beeswax before drilling each hole and take care to hold the drilling machine vertical.

HAND-SEWED SIDE STITCHING. Illus. 210 shows how to side stitch a book by hand. Sew in and out of the stab holes from head to tail, then back again. At the end of sewing, tie the ends of the thread together so that the knot can be poked down into the first stab hole.

SIDE STITCHING WITH THE SEWING AWL. (Illus. 211). Rather than use the extremely heavy, waxed nylon thread provided for this device, it is perhaps better to rewind the bobbin with No. 20 linen book thread or 4-cord polyester crochet thread. Follow the sewing directions that come with the awl. Upon reaching the end of the sewing, tie off the ends of the thread (Illus. 212). Saw a shallow cut across the back, just deep enough to bury the thread. Tie the threads together on the back side of the book so that the knot can be disposed of into the stab hole.

KNOCKING DOWN THE SEWING. Knock down the sewing by beating the threads into the paper with a mallet, then place the book between pressing boards and give it a hard squeeze in the press. Leave it there for a few minutes while you cut two $\frac{3}{8}$-inch-wide strips of paper as long as the height of the book.

Remove the book from press and glue a $\frac{3}{8}$-inch-wide strip down the back edge, rubbing the glue into the threaded stab holes with your finger: then lay on the paper strip and rub it down. Turn the book over and glue down the other strip the same way.

119

Illus. 215—The heavy-duty stabbing clamp is shown clamped to a heavy book being drilled at ¾-inch intervals for whipstitch sewing. When drilling freehand like this, with an electric drill or a hand drill, grip book and clamp in the lying press to hold it steady.

ENDPAPERS. With waxed paper on each side of the book, squeeze it again in the press while you cut and fold a pair of single-fold endpapers. Take out the book and glue a strip ¼ inch wide down the back edge and tip on the endpaper, then do the same on the other side. Place waxed paper between the book and the pressing boards and press heavily until the glue dries—45 minutes to 1 hour.

TRIMMING THE BOOK. Trim the head, tail and fore edge in the usual way, but do not attempt to round and back the book, as this is impossible where side stitching is involved.

HEADBANDING AND PADDING THE BACK. Glue headbands in place, or omit them, as desired. Pad the back with super 1½ inches shorter than the length of the back and wide enough to overhang each side 1¼ inches. Over this, glue down a piece of kraft paper the same width and long enough to cover both headbands, if any. When the glue dries, cut out the 4 corners of the paper as indicated in Illus. 213. Paper and super are to be glued together to the boards; the presence of the paper stiffens the joints enough so that, when covering, the boards are not drawn toward the back in forming the French groove, thus reducing or perhaps even losing the fore edge square.

THE LOOSE HOLLOW. The loose hollow in this case is a strip of cardboard at least $\frac{1}{16}$ inch thick, as wide as the thickness of the book *plus* the thickness of both boards, and as long as the height of the boards. Lacking proper cardboard, the loose hollow can be glued up of strips of Bristol board or heavy drawing paper to the required thickness. (The usual hollow back is loose—that is, not attached to the body of the book, being glued only to the cover material. It differs also from the loose hollow as it usually exists in binding a book of folded sections.)

BOARDING THE FLAT BACK BOOK. Cut the boards to such dimensions that the back edge is ⅜ inch in from the back edge of the book and allow for a $\frac{3}{16}$-inch square all around. Very often, too, the fore edge square is made wider than that at head and tail by as much as $\frac{1}{16}$ to ⅛ inch. If the boards should draw up in covering, the excess will take care of that and still leave a wider square at the fore edge.

To mount the boards, place a double thickness of waxed paper under the tab and glue the super down with Elmer's Glue-All (the waxed paper strips off easily when the glue is dry). Next glue the paper tab down to the super, then brush glue on the upper surface of the paper. Place the board with its back edge ⅜ inch from the back edge of the book. Lower it gently and check the squares all around. Adjust until these are satisfactory, then rub the board down over the tab and board the other side the same way. Place waxed paper between the

120

Illus. 216—The book drill provides a more accurate way to drill the back of a book for sewing. Used on thick books, it guarantees the stab holes will be straight and vertical. The inexpensive set-up shown here consists of a ¼-inch capacity electric drill fastened to a small drill stand.

book and grooving boards and press until the glue sets, at least an hour.

Cover the book with book cloth or imitation leather, cotton-backed vinyl upholstery material, or paper, using hot glue. The method of covering is as follows:

Position the book at one end of the cover material as usual, then press the loose hollow, carefully positioned, against the back of the book. Holding the end of the cloth taut, bring it around over the loose hollow and lay it on the board. Rub down the back and sides of the book as usual, turn in around the edges and make either cut corners or folded library corners. Press until the next day.

After trimming the turn-in on both boards to ⅜ inch wide, brush hot glue on the board paper and close the board on it. Treat the other board paper likewise (Illus. 214), and return to press for at least another day.

Rebinding Single-Sheet Books and Magazines

Magazines such as the *National Geographic,* the *American Artist,* and so on, are composed of single sheets, glued and side stitched with staples. Tear down such magazines as described in Chapter 2, clamp up and brush their backs with paste to soften the old glue, which you then scrape off. If the back edges are reasonably even, planing with the Surform Shaver and filing with the grit file will be sufficient. Often, however, the backs are distorted from glueing and stapling and will have to be trimmed with the guillotine or the press and plow. Trim off just as little as you have to.

Illus. 217—After the glued-up book has been drilled, divide it into sections of 16 leaves each. Using a straightedge and folder, run a crease down both sides of each section, just in front of the stab holes. This will make the book easier to open.

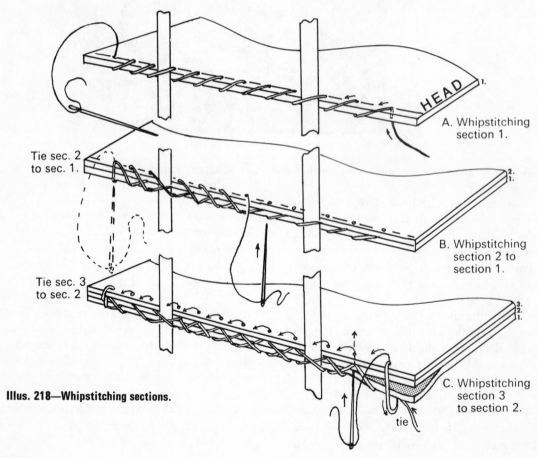

HEAD

A. Whipstitching section 1.

Tie sec. 2 to sec. 1.

B. Whipstitching section 2 to section 1.

Tie sec. 3 to sec. 2.

tie

C. Whipstitching section 3 to section 2.

Illus. 218—Whipstitching sections.

Into this same category fall books which, while being torn down, have had the folds of their sections so mutilated that repairing would add too much bulk to the back, so the folds must be trimmed off. Likewise, single-section, saddle-stitched magazines and books composed of thin sections (having few leaves, or of extremely thin paper) present so many problems in sewing and backing that it is better simply to trim off the folds and bind the book like any other composed of single sheets.

Whipstitch Method of Sewing Single Sheets

Among the several ways to bind a book of single sheets, the whipstitch method (also called oversewing) is probably the oldest and, undoubtedly, the most flexible and most secure. First examine the book or magazines to make sure there is enough width in the gutter to allow $\frac{3}{16}$ inch for the sewing.

PREPARING FOR WHIPSTITCHING. First trim or otherwise plane and smooth the back (some magazines can be bound 3 or 4 to a volume, others as many as a full year's issue). Always discard the back cover of magazines. If you can bear to part with the front covers, discard them also. Their presence only makes the book more difficult to open. The *National Geographic* puts all advertising matter on separate pages at front and back of each issue. You may discard the advertising if you wish, or bind it in with the rest of the material.

Cut two pieces of heavy, white paper, one for each side of the book. Jog the book at head and back to even the sheets and either trim with guillotine or press and plow, or shave off the unevenness, whichever may be necessary.

GLUEING UP THE BACK. Clamp the book tightly, the edges of the clamp even with the back, and brush Planatol BB or Elmer's Glue-All over the back. Wipe glue off the clamp with a damp rag.

Let the book sit 15 or 20 minutes until the glue sets.

STABBING THE BACK. In general, a book to be whipstitched is thicker and heavier than the items treated earlier on in this chapter. To make it possible to sew the book, each section will have to be stabbed or drilled. If you do not yet have a stabbing clamp, tear the book down into sections of 16 leaves each. Mark a line down the back of each section, $\frac{3}{16}$ inch from the edge. Leave $\frac{3}{4}$ inch at head and tail and mark the line for stabbing at $\frac{3}{4}$-inch intervals. Each section can then be stabbed separately with an awl.

However, the heavy duty stabbing clamp saves a great deal of time over this method of procedure. The book is first clamped in the stabbing clamp, then the whole thing in the lying press (Illus. 215). Drill completely through the book at $\frac{3}{4}$-inch intervals with a $\frac{1}{16}$-inch drill. If the book is too thick for the length of the drill, you can use a $\frac{5}{64}$-inch drill, but it is not advisable to make a larger hole than this. Where a book is far too thick for the reach of the drill, first drill as deep as the bit will go, remove the book from the clamp and tear off enough 16-leaf sections to leave only as much thickness as the drill will penetrate with a second trial.

When working a thick book, particularly, you will find it difficult to keep the drill holes perfectly straight and they will angle off in one direction or another. The book drill (Illus. 216) puts an end to this. You can buy the inexpensive arrangement shown at a mail-order house or from a firm that deals in tool specialties. It literally amounts to a drill press. In feeding the drill through thick material, drill about a half inch at a time, lifting the bit out of the hole after each plunge to clear it of paper shavings.

When tearing the drilled book down into 16-leaf sections, do *not* count the white sheet on each side as one of the leaves.

SEWING THE WHIPSTITCH. Once the book has been torn down, prepare the sections for sewing by creasing each one on both sides, just in front of the stab holes, to make the book open more easily (Illus. 217).

Illus. 218 shows the way to sew the whipstitch. Starting with section 1 at A, simply pass the needle upward through each stab hole in succession, from head to tail.

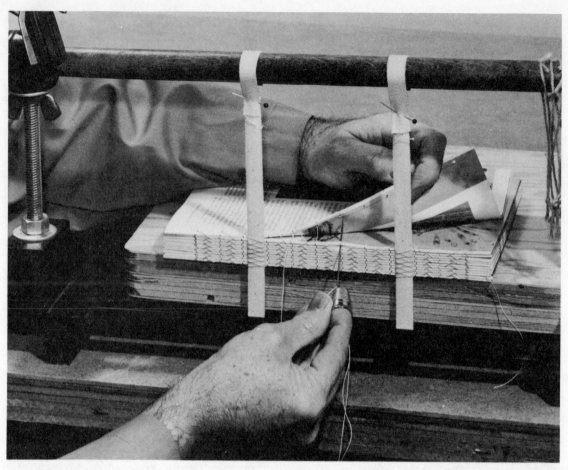

Illus. 219—Sewing the whipstitched book on tapes. Lifting of the top section is exaggerated for purpose of demonstration.

Then lay the second section on and pass the needle upward through the last stab hole of each section, then around over the back and up through the stab holes again. This locks the two sections together. Then continue sewing toward the head, passing the needle upward through the corresponding stab holes in each section. At the last stab hole, lay the third section on, pass the needle upward through all three sections, then over the back and back up through the same stab hole again, as shown at C. Continue sewing then toward the tail, whip-stitching section 3 to section 2. Illus. 219 very clearly shows how the needle is passed through one section below and then through the one

on top. Each time you lay a new section on, pass the needle through the last three sections (including the new one) for a tie, then continue sewing by whipstitching the new section to the last one down. As you sometimes have to pinch the needle pretty tightly, it is a good idea to use a thimble.

Instead of sewing on tapes as shown, the book may be sewed on buried cords.

At the conclusion of sewing, knock down the swell, jog the book as even as possible at the back, and give it a hard squeeze in the press overnight to bury the threads in the paper. Next, paste up the first and last two or three sections in the same way described for a book of

Illus. 220—In pasting the cloth joint to the book, let it overlap ¾ inch in from the back edge.

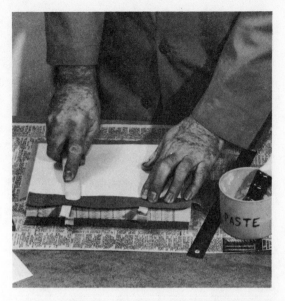

folded sections. Do not at this time apply any more glue to the back of the book. Cut two ⅜-inch-wide strips of paper and glue one down to each side, along the back edge, covering the exposed stitching.

THE CLOTH JOINT. Cut two strips of unbleached muslin, or unbleached linen artists' canvas, or cotton duck, or Holland, or similar cloth, as long (warpwise) as the height of the book and 2½ inches wide. If the material you have is flabby (lacking size or filler), stiffen it with starch. Ready-prepared or spray starch will do. Soak the material with starch, wipe off the excess, then iron the cloth dry. For extra stiffness, repeat the starching and iron a time or two until the cloth feels like it has body.

Paste the cloth strips down on each side of the book, overlapping the back edge ¾ inch, and rub down with a folder (Illus. 220–221).

Next, cut two sheets of white endpaper, or drawing paper, each the same height as the book but ¼ inch less in width. Brush paste on one side of the sheet and rub it down over the flyleaf, overlapping the cloth joint ½ inch (Illus. 221–222). Paste the other sheet down the same way on the other side of the book. Place waxed paper on both sides of each pair of pasted sheets, put between plain pressing boards and press heavily until the following day.

ROUNDING AND BACKING THE WHIPSTITCHED BOOK. Jog the head and the back of the book

Illus. 220—In pasting the cloth joint to the book, let it overlap ¾ inch in from the back edge.

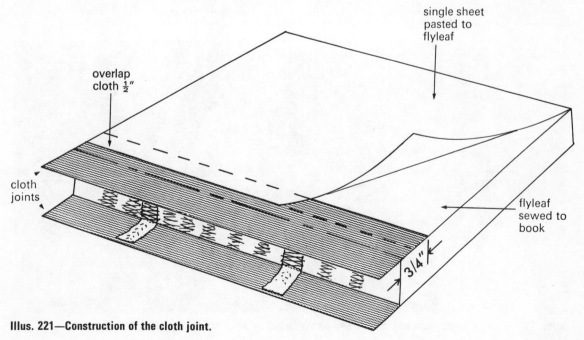

overlap cloth ½"

single sheet pasted to flyleaf

cloth joints

flyleaf sewed to book

¾"

Illus. 221—Construction of the cloth joint.

flat, clamp up and brush on a coat of Planatol BB or Elmer's Glue-All. When tacky, remove from the clamp, bind the book with tape to hold it in shape and trim the fore edge with press and plow.

The next step is to round the back, but do not try for too much of a round. Back the book with a $\frac{3}{16}$-inch-deep backing groove with the free flaps of the cloth joints outside the backing boards. Take care in backing, too, not to hit the threads too hard.

Cut a piece of super long enough to reach from the lockstitches at the head to those at the tail and wide enough to provide a $1\frac{1}{4}$-inch tab on each side of the book. Glue up the back, rub down the super, then brush more glue over the super and fill in between the tapes with heavy kraft paper. Also glue kraft paper over the super at the head and tail, but leave enough room for trimming and glueing down the headbands. Leave the book in press until the glue is dry.

TRIMMING HEAD AND TAIL OF THE WHIP-STITCHED BOOK. Trim the head and tail "out of boards," as described in Chapter 9. Instead of using the book's own boards, however, use a pair of plywood boards $\frac{1}{4}$- or $\frac{3}{8}$-inch-thick to provide room for folding the super tab and the cloth joint back out of the way, behind the

book. Trim off the free end of the cloth joint even with the trim line.

Cut and glue on the head- and tailband, then construct the 3-part hollow back described in Chapter 10 and glue it on the back.

COVERING AND PASTING DOWN THE WHIP-STITCHED BOOK. Board and cover the book in the French groove style (Chapter 10), using plain boards. Slip a doubled sheet of waxed paper under the tab, brush glue on the cloth joint and press down the tapes. Brush glue on the tapes, then rub the super into contact all along. Brush on another coat of Elmer's Glue-All and place the back edge of the board along the backing groove and lower it into place, checking the squares all around to make sure they are correct. Cover with waxed paper, turn the book over, and mount the other board the same way. Press between grooving boards until the glue is dry.

Cover the book with any of the materials in any of the styles previously described, including leather over false bands, if you wish. The final step is to cut the board paper, a single sheet which may be of a different color than the flyleaf, and paste it or glue it down (whichever is required) so as to leave $\frac{1}{4}$ inch of the cloth joint exposed on the board (Illus. 223–224).

Illus. 222—Paste a single sheet and rub it down on the flyleaf so as to overlap the cloth joint $\frac{1}{2}$ inch.

Illus. 223—Glue the single-sheet board paper down in such a way as to leave $\frac{1}{4}$ inch of the cloth joint exposed on the board.

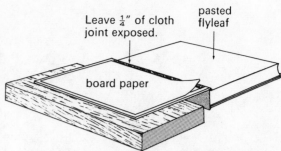

Illus. 224—Glueing down board paper with cloth joint.

Perfect Binding

"Perfect" is not a qualitative name or attribute but a description of the method of binding, which was developed around the start of the 20th century as a final means of making single-sheet binding commercially profitable. For centuries, binders had tried one unsuccess-ful method after another to bind single sheets without sewing. Perfect binding came into vogue as the only method for binding catalogs, telephone books and, when the paperback book was revived in the 1930's, it was resorted to as being the most economical and satisfactory method of binding for cheap books. However,

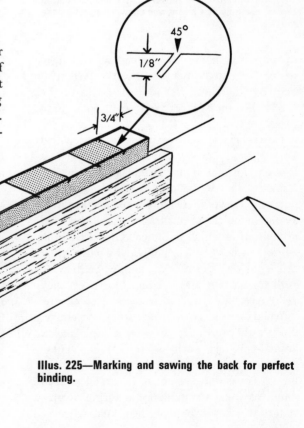

Illus. 225—Marking and sawing the back for perfect binding.

127

Illus. 226—Cardboards on each side of sheaf of paper stiffens the back edge with $\frac{1}{4}$ inch protruding above the clamp for sawing. Saw cuts are made at a 45° angle in alternate directions. If you are not good at judging angles, use a guide like the one shown supporting the saw.

in spite of its name, the method was far from perfect, and anybody over 40 can well remember how the catalogs and paperbacks of the 1930's shed their leaves like trees in an autumn gale.

However, research conducted during World War II and during the subsequent decades brought to light many formulas for superior, resinous glues to be used for a multitude of purposes. One of these is polyvinyl acetate glue, available under various trade names, the most ubiquitous of which is Elmer's Glue-All. Milk white and fairly thick, polyvinyl acetate glues brush out well, dry quickly, and, when dry, are both transparent and flexible. Moreover, they yield reasonably well to water and so can be softened and scraped away when necessary, though they are not so good at this as an animal product such as hide glue. These attributes make this type of glue ideal for glueing up books that are not to be sewed and, in some cases, even suitable for covering, a procedure which will be described later.

128

Early in this century, a perfect binding machine was developed that produced an improved perfect binding, though at the expense of thrift; it was therefore used only for certain types of editions. The machine made diagonal cuts in the back of the book, then forced glue and strong threads into the cuts. The protruding ends of the threads were subsequently glued down to the sides of the book, securely locking them in place. A book so made cannot come apart, and so this is the method which has been adapted to hand bookbinding. Its advantages are that the book can either have flat or rounded back, and it can be more quickly produced than a book sewed by the whipstitch method, or some other of the methods that have been introduced.

PREPARING THE BOOK FOR PERFECT BINDING. Thickness is not taken into account in perfect binding. The book may contain few or many pages. Where the pages are few, the back is left flat. Where the pages are many, the back may be left flat, but is usually rounded and backed.

Books suitable for perfect binding are saddle-stitched magazines with their folds trimmed off, books with mutilated section folds that have had to be trimmed, and single sheets of typewritten or printed paper.

Illus. 227—You really only need one kind of reinforcement in the saw cuts, but a choice is shown here of, left to right: linen twine, rayon embroidery thread, nylon twine, polyester crochet thread. The glue, Planatol BB, is a product of West Germany, made especially for single-sheet binding. Elmer's Glue-All is a satisfactory substitute.

Assemble the sheets in proper order (a process called "collating"), jog the sheaf as even as possible at head and back, then trim the back edge with the guillotine or the press and plow. Typing paper or the like can usually be clamped up and scraped with the Surform Shaver as described earlier on. The main thing to watch for is that each and every sheet has its back edge exposed to the glue.

MARKING THE BACK FOR PERFECT BINDING. Clamp the book in the glueing clamp, the back level with the bars. Brush Planatol BB or Elmer's Glue-All on the back. In 15 to 20 minutes, when the glue is dry, drop the clamp $\frac{1}{8}$ inch and mark the back with 3 or 4 pairs of lines (depending on the height of the book), starting $\frac{3}{4}$ inch from head and tail. The pairs of lines are set about $1\frac{1}{4}$ inches apart, and the spaces between pairs may be measured out roughly equal.

Cut two pieces of waste cardboard, such as the backs of drawing paper pads, the same size as the book. Stand the book on its spine and loosen the clamp screws; then insert a cardboard on each side of the book, level with its back, and reclamp.

SAWING THE BACK FOR PERFECT BINDING. Grip the fore edge of the book in the lying press

(Illus. 225–226) with a $\frac{1}{4}$-inch lift under each end of the clamp. Screw up the lying press hand tight, remove the lifts and let the clamp drop, then retighten the screws. The back now protrudes $\frac{1}{4}$ inch above the clamp bars, allowing plenty of room for sawing. The cardboard on each side of the sheaf holds the leaves firm so that they will not tear while being sawed.

Use a tenon or dovetail saw, and it is best if it has 15 or more teeth to the inch and a blade thickness of 0.02 inch (0.508 mm). A coping saw blade is almost this thin (0.023-inch), and can be used on relatively thin books, but is not recommended for thick ones on account of the flexibility of the coping saw blade.

Sawing for perfect binding is conducted differently than other kinds of back sawing utilized in bookbinding. The sawcuts are made at an angle of 45° to the back (Illus. 226). The first saw cut at the head is made with the blade leaning toward the head; the second with the blade leaning toward the tail; the third toward the head, the fourth toward the tail, and so on, alternating the direction of the angle with each cut. The vertical depth of the sawcut should be about $\frac{1}{8}$ inch (Illus. 225).

REINFORCING THE BACK. Various materials can be used for the "strong threads" provided

129

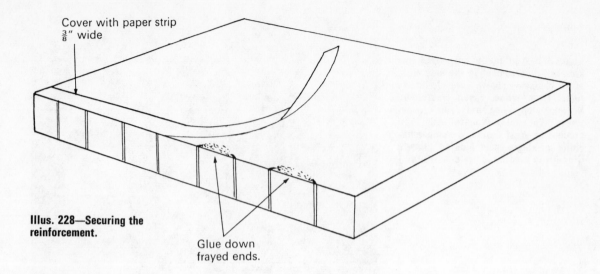

Cover with paper strip
$\frac{3}{8}''$ wide

Illus. 228—Securing the reinforcement.

Glue down
frayed ends.

by the perfect binding machine. Never in history have so many suitable materials been available to the bookbinder. Where once only a linen twine would do, now you may use nylon twine, nylon or orlon-nylon yarn, rayon embroidery thread, nylon or polyester crochet thread, etc. Use these materials in bundles of 2 to half a dozen, according to their size, or a single length of linen sewing cord. Brush glue into a saw cut, force the reinforcement into it with the edge of a thin folder or a table knife, then brush more glue on top. When you have filled all the sawcuts (Illus. 227), brush glue over the entire back of the book, filling the saw cuts level.

Avoid cotton, sisal or jute twine for this purpose, as well as any other that is stiff and brittle.

Synthetic fibres have the advantage of not only being strong and flexible, but also practically indestructible by time. They will undoubtedly outlast the book itself.

As soon as the glue has set, cut off the protruding ends of the threads about a half inch or less long.

Securing the Reinforcement. Unravel the threads against a piece of sheet metal with the point of an awl, then scrape them out to fine, frayed ends with the edge of a knife. Glue the frayed ends down to the outside of the book, the

frayed fans parallel to the back edge, and those of each pair pointing toward each other (Illus. 228). Cover with waxed paper and knock the threads down with a hammer, then turn the book over and glue down the threads on the other side and knock them down with light hammering. Place the book between plain pressing boards and give it a hard squeeze in the press to further embed the threads. Do not squeeze the book so hard as to make the back go concave.

Strip off the waxed paper and cover the glued-down ends with a $\frac{3}{8}$-inch-wide strip of paper on each side, along the back edge (Illus. 228). You will benefit by using 100 per cent rag bond paper for this (parchment typing paper); or, at least, a 25 per cent rag bond. Brush Elmer's Glue-All on the strip, then rub it down in place. Treat both sides of the book the same. Place waxed paper between the book and pressing boards and set aside under a brick to dry.

Endpapers. Cut a pair of sheets from 70-lb offset or drawing paper and fold them with the grain to make single-fold endpapers. Glue a $\frac{1}{4}$-inch-wide strip down the back edge of the book and tip on an endpaper and rub it down with a folder. Tip on the other endpaper and place again under a board and brick until dry.

Subsequent Steps of Forwarding. Trim the

130

book in your usual way. Do not round and back, as the back is to be left flat.

Glue on headbands and pad the back with super and kraft paper as described for the side-stitched book (Illus. 213). Board and cover as desired. Instead of tipped-on endpapers, you may use the cloth joint described in binding the whipstitched book.

SPECIALTY COVER MATERIALS. You are not confined to use of professional book covering materials, such as leather, buckram, book cloth, and so on. In recent years, many new products have become available that the amateur book-binder can readily turn to use. You may cover a book with printed cotton cloth, with printed or plain cotton duck, artists' canvas of unbleached linen, hair canvas, bark cloth, denim in any of its solid colors and handsome prints, or any other fabric, even thin silk, velvet or velveteen, suitable for making blank-book diaries. There is only one requirement for printed or colored cloth. It must be colorfast.

SELF-ADHESIVE PLASTIC AND LINING PAPERS. These come in rolls and are used for decorative purposes to cover shelving, cabinets, chests, and so on. The self-adhesive plastics require only that the paper backing be stripped away, before the material is rubbed down in place on the book. Since the adhesive side will not stick to itself, the material is remarkably easy to handle (Illus. 229). The plastic wears well, looks nice, and is an inexpensive cover material for manuscripts, reports, music, club minutes, etc. Use non-warping paste or hot glue on the board papers to avoid warping the boards.

If you plan in advance to use water-base paste on the board papers, before covering the book, line the boards on the *outside* with newspaper and water-base paste and press until dry. The pasted sheet on the outside will counteract the pull of the pasted board paper inside.

Useful for siding quarter bindings and half bindings are many colorful patterns of non-adhesive, plastic-finished lining paper, also available in rolls. It may be adhered to the boards with any of the adhesives you normally use in bookbinding, as well as with vinyl wallpaper paste (a ready-mixed paste available at

Illus. 229—Many patterns of self-adhesive decorative plastic, as well as plastic-coated lining paper, are available. These make good siding material to be used with book cloth, buckram, or imitation leather. Two patterns of self-adhesive plastic are being used here for a quarter binding on boards.

131

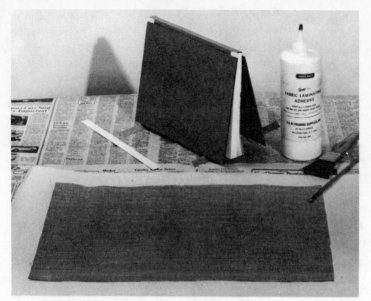

Illus. 230—You can glue the outer surfaces of both boards at once if you stand the book on its fore edge like this. Or, you can glue and cover one board at a time when covering with plain fabric. Elmer's Glue-All may be used instead of the fabric laminating adhesive shown. Foreground: Cover material of hair canvas (contains 18% goat hair). It has been treated with Scotchgard and ironed flat.

paint and wallpaper stores), which is customarily used for applying vinyl-coated wallpaper and other paper and fabric wall coverings.

COVERING WITH FABRIC. When covering a book with ordinary cloth, the procedure is altered because the untreated cloth would let the glue soak through and spoil its appearance. Therefore, instead of applying the glue to the cloth, brush it on the book instead.

Almost any cloth will benefit, however, from a treatment with Scotchgard, particularly those of light weight and light in color. Heavy canvas, such as found on ledgers and similar blank books, can be used without such treatment if desired. Scotchgard is the trade name of a product available everywhere in variety stores and shops and department stores where yard goods are sold. It comes in a spray can to be used on garments and upholstered furniture to render the cloth water-, dirt-, and grease-repellent. A fabric treated with Scotchgard can be wiped clean with a damp rag.

Do not lay the cloth out on newspaper for treatment, as it may pick up the ink when wet. Place it on clean wrapping paper over a cushion of newspapers. Cut the cloth to size and spray it in accordance with the instructions on the can. Scotchgard will not discolor nor change the appearance of the cloth nor cause it to shrink. Three hours after spraying, iron the cloth flat and it is ready for glueing to the book.

The glue to use is Elmer's Glue-All or any other polyvinyl acetate glue. The fabric-laminating adhesive shown in Illus. 230 is a variant formula of this type of glue, being waterproof when dry.

If you like to work fast, stand the book on its fore edge as in Illus. 230 and brush the glue all over the outer surface of both boards, over the edges and into the French grooves. Do not brush glue on the spine, but brush glue on one side of the loose hollow (the light strip to the left of the book in the photo). Let the book stand until the glue turns tacky—and keep an electric iron handy, turned to medium heat. Position the book at one end of the laid-out cloth, allowing ¾ inch all around for the turn-in. Place the loose hollow against the back, sticky side out, and bring the cloth over it and down on the top board and rub it down through a sheet of paper to protect the cloth.

If the glue is too fluid, it will seep through the cloth. If it is too dry, the cloth will not stick. Just make sure it is not too fluid. Where the cloth fails to stick, iron it down through a piece of wrapping paper to avoid scorching the

Illus. 231—Here is the third hand you need when glueing for the turn-in and turning in the cloth around the boards. You could also use the sawing clamp. Note that the back is lifted off the table so that the cloth can be turned in under the headband.

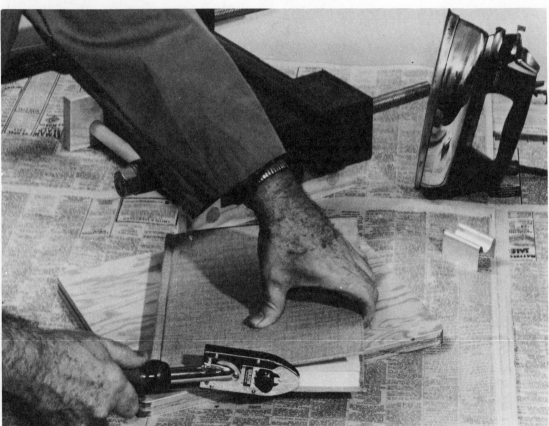

Illus. 232—The dry-mount tacking iron is a device used by photographers to hold a photo in place while it is being readied for the dry mounting press. Its small size and ease of handling make it ideal for applying heat to adhere the edges of the boards to the cloth as well as in the French grooves. The electric iron (background) is used to iron the faces of the boards, ensuring adhesion.

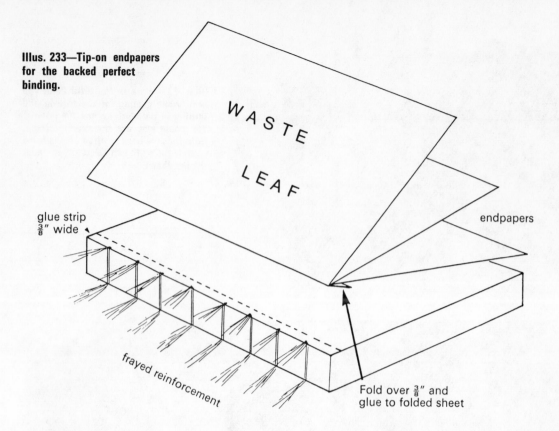

Illus. 233—Tip-on endpapers for the backed perfect binding.

WASTE

LEAF

glue strip
⅜" wide

endpapers

frayed reinforcement

Fold over ⅜" and
glue to folded sheet

cloth. The heat reactivates the glue and it will take proper hold.

If you prefer to work more slowly and surely, glue up only one board at a time and cover the book as you go.

Illus. 231 shows how to hold the book in the end of a bench press (or, you can use the glueing clamp), so that the inside edges of the boards can be glued up for the turn-in. Grip the book so that the back is lifted, allowing room to turn in the cloth under the headband.

Since cloth has a tendency to ravel at the edges, and will do so if you make cut corners, it is best to provide library corners, folding the cloth over on itself and applying more glue where needed.

Iron down the turn-in and take especial care along the edges of the boards and in the French grooves. The dry-mount tacking iron (available at a photographic supply house) is ideal for this job on account of its small size and ease of handling (Illus. 232). If you are using a steam iron, do not turn it on its side unless you are absolutely certain that the reservoir is empty, or you will get water all over your work.

When the book is fully covered, put a sheet of aluminum flashing between each board and the book, with waxed paper over the metal to protect it from the glue. Press heavily between grooving boards for at least an hour to set the cloth well into the glue. While the book is in press, shape the corners of the spine with a pointed folder.

An alternative method of working is to let the glue dry thoroughly on the book, then lay on the cloth and iron it on. It is a good idea to put a sheet of clean paper between the iron and the cloth.

After trimming out the turn-in, stick down the board papers with Elmer's Glue-All, hot glue, or non-warping paste, preferably either of the last two. Press until the book is entirely dry, or until the boards no longer have a tendency, on sitting, to bow outward.

134

Rounding and Backing the Perfect Binding

Forward the book as described in preceding paragraphs for the flat-back perfect binding, to the point where the threads are glued into the saw cuts in the back of the book. Cut them off to a length of 1¼ inches. Unravel the threads with the point of an awl against a piece of sheet metal, then fray them out with the rounded point of a knife blade. These will provide extra strength for the cover joints. Hammer the threads lightly at the point of emergence from the book to flatten them.

Make two folded endpapers the size of the book, then cut a single sheet for each, the same height but ⅜ inch wider, and fold over the ⅜-inch excess (Illus. 233). Brush Elmer's Glue-All on the inside of the fold-over, insert the folded edge of the endpaper, and rub down with a folder. Make both sets of endpapers the same. Draw the frayed cords out of the way, behind the book (Illus. 233); then brush glue on a strip ⅜ inch wide down the back edge of the book and rub the endpaper down in place, folded edge even with the back edge of the book. The ⅜-inch-wide fold-over goes next to the book; the single sheet is on the outside, as a waste leaf. After glueing on both endpapers, set the book aside under a board and a brick for 10 or 15 minutes, then trim the head, tail, and fore edge as usual.

Before the glue becomes fully set, round the back, but do not try for too much roundness, as the perfect binding style does not allow for much. Mark the waste leaves for a 3/16-inch-deep backing groove and back the book. Brush paste on the glued back and let soften, then scrape

Illus. 234—Note how the paper tab has been doubled back and glued down over the super and the frayed reinforcement. The imitation leather cover, put on with hot glue, requires no board lining and the board paper is glued down with the same glue.

135

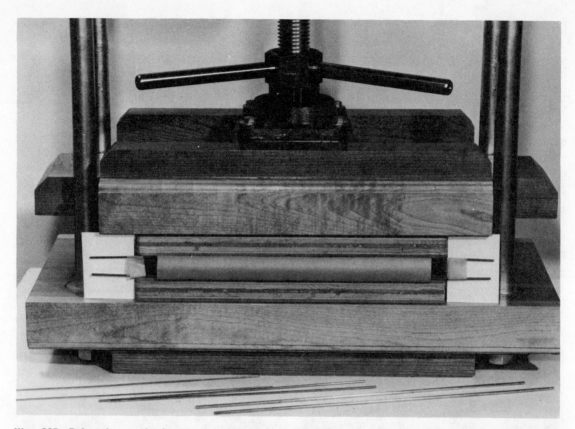

Illus. 235—Before the grooving board was invented, old-time binders used a pair of brass rods in the French grooves to shape them, held in place by pressing boards. A modern adaptation to make the rods more manageable is to wrap masking tape around the ends to keep the rods from jumping out of the grooves. Use $\frac{3}{32}$-inch bronze welding rod from a welding supply house. Use $\frac{1}{16}$ inch for thinner boards, $\frac{1}{8}$ inch for thicker. Keep a few lengths on hand for an emergency when all your grooving boards are in use.

down to avoid too much glue build-up. When dry, glue on head- and tailbands and super backing in the space between, 1¼-inch-wide tab on each side.

Make a 3-part hollow back (Chapter 10) of single-ply kid Bristol or heavy kraft or drawing paper, long enough to cover both headbands and as wide as the back measured over the curve. Brush a fresh coat of glue over the entire back, position the middle section of the hollow back and rub it down thoroughly to ensure adhesion. Fold over one side, brush it with a thin coat of Elmer's Glue-All, then fold the other side over on top of it and rub it down. Leave the book between the backing boards, or transfer it to the book press, until the following day.

Cut the waste leaf on each side down to a tab the same length as the super but twice its width. Glue the frayed cords down to the paper tab, then glue the super down on top of them. Brush again with glue and fold the paper tab back over the super to the turn-up of the backing groove and rub it down. Brush glue on the paper tab, replace the protective newspaper under the tab with waxed paper, and set the board so that the squares are even all around and there is space for a French groove.

Turn the book over and glue up the tab and set the board in the same way. Place waxed paper between the book and grooving boards and press under heavy pressure until the glue is firmly set.

Cover with any material, in any style that

suits you. Trim out the turn-in to $\frac{3}{8}$ inch wide and glue down the board papers (if glue was used to adhere the cover material) (Illus. 234).

Instead of using the endpapers described above, you can provide the book with cloth joints, as described earlier in this chapter. In this case, the book is then boarded and covered and the job is concluded by sticking down single-sheet board papers, which are so cut and so placed as to leave $\frac{1}{4}$ inch of the cloth joint exposed along the back edge of the board.

If you should some day have all your grooving boards in use and have need of another pair, you can do as the old-timers did in customary practice, as shown in Illus. 235.

Illus. 236—Finished books, showing printed, gilded and foil-lettered titling. The title for the book of Bewick woodcuts, being far too long for the 3 × 5 hand press, was printed with the arrangement shown in Illus. 241, in the screw-type book press shown in Illus. 2.

14. Finishing

"Finishing" means the titling and decorating of a book after it has been bound. It may consist of as little as a single-word title on the spine, or of as much as a profusion of blind and gold tooling in an intricate pattern over the spine or backbone and covers that takes many hours of careful work to execute.

For the amateur, the simplest, quickest and easiest way to title a book is to letter the title and the author's name on a slip of paper in black or colored drawing ink. Then cut the slip to fit on the spine of the book and glue it on with Elmer's Glue-All. Sometimes, a larger title, on a larger piece of paper, is glued to the front cover.

The title may also be typewritten and glued on (Illus. 202).

Choose a colored or toned paper that goes well with the color of the binding. Paper can be toned by soaking it in a watercolor solution of acrylic paint and water. This is waterproof when dry, and the paper can be wetted again and dried between blotters to flatten it.

When cutting a paper slip for a title, make sure that the grain in the paper runs vertically. If the paper is thick, turn it over on a smooth surface and feather the edges with No. 120 grit garnet paper. Use only a small piece of cabinet paper and fold it double. Hold the title slip securely and sand lightly in one direction only along the edge. If you scrub back and forth, you are likely to crumple the paper and have it all to do over again.

The Foil Writing Pen. This is the well known woodburning pen. Every set contains at least one screw-on point designed for writing over gold, silver, or colored foil.

The first step is to letter the title on a thin piece of paper in pencil. Insert the book in the lying press with the head tilted upward and a thin piece of cardboard on each side to protect the covers. Cut a piece of foil to size and attach it to the backbone with masking tape. Tape the lettering pattern on over the foil (Illus. 237).

Carefully letter in the title with the hot, foil-writing pen (Illus. 238). After the foil has been removed, go over any letters that have been filled in, with the point of a pen-knife, scraping away the excess color. In the same way, lines that waver or have become too thick can be straightened out or thinned by light scraping. Tiny spots of color that resist the knife point can be picked out with a needle.

Printing Book Titles. A little hand press like the one in Illus. 239 and 240 is ideal for printing titles, using regular foundry type. You

Illus. 237—Lettering pattern taped to back of book, ready for lining in with the foil-writing pen. The thin paper title is taped on over foil—in this case, "silver" foil. The cardboards on either side of the book protect the covers from being creased by clamping in the press.

Illus. 238—Little skill is required to title a book with the foil-writing pen. However, practice first on scrap material or old books to learn how fast or slow to move the pen and how much or little pressure to apply.

Illus. 239—A small hand press like this provides the easiest and neatest method of titling books. Print the title on a slip of paper, which you then glue to the book. This little press has a chase measuring 3 × 5 inches, but it is not a toy. It is a real printing press and can print beautiful titles.

Illus. 240—The book title has been proofed on paper slips of different colors, to see which goes best with the cover material. Note the title form locked up in the chase.

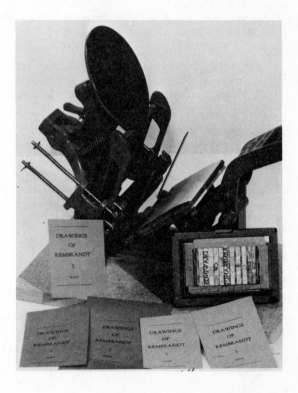

140

Illus. 241—This wooden chase was made for printing type forms, lino blocks and woodcuts with the screw-type book press (Illus. 2). The 12-inch lengths of 12-point lead rule on either side of the type form distribute the platen pressure for proper printing. This same set-up can also be used for printing titles with a rolling pin.

need several sizes of cap fonts (fonts of capital letters) and quads and spaces. Choose a size and style of type that goes with the size and subject matter of the book. The titles shown in Illus. 240 were printed with a Roman style, 18-point type called Forum. The author's name is in 14-point Centaur caps. Capital letters are generally used for titling, though sometimes lower case (small letters) is also used, following a capital letter at the beginning of the word.

To print titles, you will need type in any case, but you can also turn your screw-type book press into a printing press similar to the kind used in Benjamin Franklin's day. Illus. 241 shows how a wooden chase (type holder) can be made and the type locked up in it for printing with the screw press (Illus. 2). Roll out the ink on a piece of glass, using a brayer (ink roller) about 4 inches wide. The kind sold at

art supply stores for block printing is satisfactory. Run the inked roller over the type, then lay on a sheet of printing paper and another piece of soft paper on top. Then lay on a sheet of red press board or thin cardboard.

Cut a piece of ¼-inch tempered hardboard to fit into the press and rest on the springs in each corner of the bed. Then bring the platen (the hardboard in this case) down and squeeze it against the paper on the type. A few practice attempts will teach you how much pressure to apply—start with very little.

Illus. 242 shows the same arrangement. If you have a steel bookbinding press, or other press without springs in the corners of the bed, you can install the springs directly in the corners of the chase and lay the sheet of hardboard on top before inserting in the press.

The purpose of the springs is to control the

141

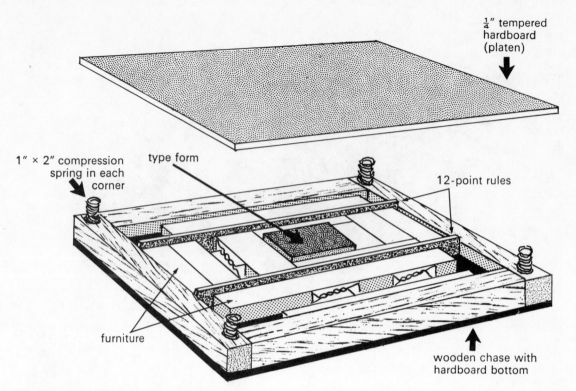

Illus. 242—Type lock-up for printing a book title.

descent of the platen, which otherwise would swing and knock the paper askew.

If no screw-press is available, go back to the arrangement in Illus. 241. Lay on the paper as explained above. (In all cases, the printing and backing paper and the press board must be large enough to cover not only the type form but also the "rails" of 12-point rule on either side.) With a slow, steady motion, roll the rolling pin from one end of the rails to the other, applying a little pressure. A rolling pin with ball-bearing handles is best for this. After a few trials, you will have the knack well in hand.

If you do not know how to set type or lock up a form, visit your public library. You are sure to find a number of books there on the subject of amateur printing that will provide you with all the information you need.

Once you have printed several title slips for a book (extras in case of accident), do not sand the edges or glue a slip to the book until the

following day, so as to allow sufficient time for the ink to become thoroughly dry. In glueing down, apply a thin coat of Elmer's to the back of the slip, position it, rub down lightly with your fingers, then cover with a sheet of blank paper and rub down with a bone folder.

TITLES BY TOOLING. Tooling involves the use of a hot tool with which to impress a letter or a design into the cover material of the book. Such tools are usually made of brass, fitted with a wooden handle.

"Blind" tooling is any kind of lettering or lining in which the tool alone is used on the cover material, leaving a blank impression that is darker in color than the surrounding material.

The only tooling of interest to the beginning amateur is titling, running lines across the backbone, and, occasionally, imprinting a small design stamp, which may be made from a piece of ½-inch square or round brass rod, or which may be a design cast in foundry type and available in fonts containing a number of designs of different point sizes.

THE LINING PALLET. You can purchase or you can make your own lining pallets from $\frac{1}{8}$-inch-thick sheet brass (Illus. 245, 246, 249, 250, 251).

With two pallets about 3 inches wide, one that strikes a line $\frac{1}{16}$ inch wide and the other a $\frac{1}{32}$-inch line, you can work out a number of combinations of lines at head and tail, and/or above and below the title.

GOLD TOOLING. Gold tooling is accomplished two ways, with pure, beaten gold leaf or with gold foil. Foil also is available in imitation gold as well as imitation silver and various colors of bronzing powder. Always use either gold leaf or real gold foil on leather. Imitation gold will turn green and scaly in time. The imitation and colored foils can be used on all other cover materials.

Gold leaf is rather difficult to handle. It is so light, the slightest breeze will blow it away, so hold in your breath when working with it. Keep doors and windows closed to avoid drafts.

Lay the booklet of gold leaves on the gold cushion, which has been dusted with pumice powder. Slip a greaseless knife blade under the first leaf you open to and carefully transfer the gold leaf to the cushion. Set the book aside, lean over the gold leaf and *lightly* breathe on it to make it lie flat. Using the gold knife in a sawing manner, cut off pieces of gold leaf to fit the title space (Illus. 244).

Dip a piece of cotton in a solution of half white vinegar and half water ($2\frac{1}{2}$ per cent acetic acid solution). Wipe this over the space that is to receive the title. Let it dry.

GLAIR. (Also spelled "glaire.") You can make

Illus. 243—Gold stamping supplies. Mesh balls next to the Vaseline are plastic (behind) and copper pot cleaners used for scraping away excess gold leaf after stamping. V is a 50—50 solution of vinegar and water; G is for glair. Gold leaf comes in a booklet containing 25 leaves, $3\frac{3}{8}$ inches square. Foil comes in rolls, as it is usually used with a gold-stamping machine. The smaller rolls are 200-ft. rolls of imitation gold; the larger, 200-ft. rolls of real gold. Real gold foil is 0.002-inch (0.0508mm) thick, and imitation gold foil is only 0.001-inch (0.0254mm) thick.

your own glair by decanting the white of a large egg into a sauce dish. Add about half as much vinegar and whip together with a fork until it gets frothy. Do this the day before you plan to do gold stamping. Let the glair stand overnight, then strain it into a small jar. When you are finished with the day's gilding, throw out the remainder of glair.

In America, professional bookbinders use "blood albumen" for a size. This comes in the form of dried crystals. To one teaspoonful of crystals add 4 of water and one of vinegar; stir

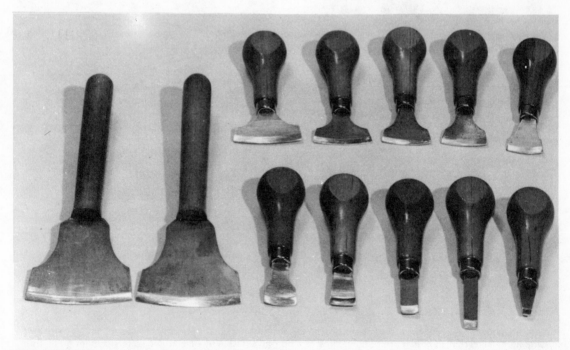

Illus. 245—Home-made lining pallets of $\frac{1}{8}$-inch-thick brass, for making lines $\frac{1}{16}$ inch wide, from $\frac{1}{4}$ inch to $3\frac{3}{8}$ inches long. The large liners at the left are for making $\frac{1}{32}$ and $\frac{1}{16}$ inch lines, respectively. These two are all you really need for putting blind or gold lines on book backs.

144

thoroughly and let stand overnight. If need be, strain it before use—usually it is well liquefied and does not need straining.

THE LETTERING PALLET. (Illus. 247). The lettering pallet is commercially available in three sizes—for stamping lines 5-, 6-, and 7-inches long. It is an expensive device, costing over twice as much as the small hand press in Illus. 240, but is almost a practical necessity for stamping titles in gold. However, you can make use of the single-letter pallet (Illus. 247, 248) to stamp the title letters one at a time.

THE FINISHING STOVE. (Illus. 249). A single or double electric hot plate furnishes the heat for the tools. The heat source may also be gas, either city gas or bottled gas. Heat the tools slowly. That way, they come to temperature all over at the same time. If you heat them too fast, they will heat unevenly, which can cause trouble in the stamping (Illus. 249).

THE COOLING PAD. (Illus. 250). The lining tool must be neither too hot nor too cool for successful stamping. Heat it until a drop of water sizzles on the metal, then cool the tool by laying it on a saturated towel in a pan. Cool evenly by turning the tool over quickly and

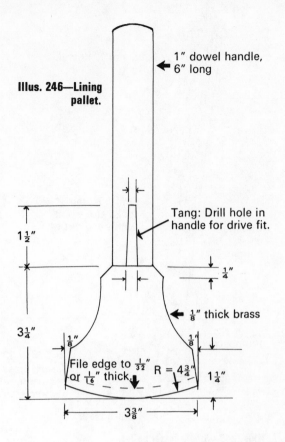

Illus. 246—Lining pallet.

1" dowel handle, 6" long

Tang: Drill hole in handle for drive fit.

$1\frac{1}{2}$"

$3\frac{1}{4}$"

$\frac{1}{4}$"

$\frac{1}{8}$" thick brass

$\frac{1}{8}$"

$\frac{1}{8}$"

File edge to $\frac{1}{32}$" or $\frac{1}{16}$" thick.

R = $4\frac{3}{4}$"

$1\frac{1}{4}$"

$3\frac{3}{8}$"

Illus. 247—Lettering pallets. The commercial model at the left, made by W. O. Hickok Mfg. Co., will stamp a line of type 5 inches long. Turning the thumbscrews at the ends causes the clamping blocks to move toward or away from each other, so that the type is always centered under the handle. Single-letter or ornament-stamping pallets are unavailable commercially, but are easy to make from the specifications in Illus. 248.

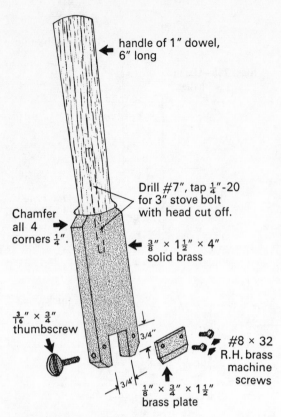

handle of 1" dowel, 6" long

Chamfer all 4 corners $\frac{1}{4}$".

Drill #7", tap $\frac{1}{4}$"-20 for 3" stove bolt with head cut off.

$\frac{3}{8}$" × $1\frac{1}{2}$" × 4" solid brass

$\frac{3}{16}$" × $\frac{3}{4}$" thumbscrew

3/4"

3/4"

$\frac{1}{8}$" × $\frac{3}{4}$" × $1\frac{1}{2}$" brass plate

#8 × 32 R.H. brass machine screws

Illus. 248—Single-letter pallet.

perhaps back again. Do not cool until the steam stops hissing. The tool is then too cold. Practice until you can stop just before the tool stops hissing.

THE WIPING PAD. (Illus. 250). This is a small block of plywood padded with cotton and covered with suede leather or with any leather with the flesh side out. Wipe the marking end of the tool on the pad to remove any possible dirt and moisture.

BLIND-TOOLING THE BANDS. (Illus. 251). One heating will not be enough to run a blind line on either side of all the bands. Reheat the tool as soon as it cools down too far and continue with blinding in the lines. Do not tool blind lines in the space at the top reserved for the title. These lines will be run in gold.

TITLING EQUIPMENT. An entire line of type can be set up in the lettering pallet. Also avail-

Illus. 249—The finishing stove, used to heat the tools for blind or gold stamping. It consists of a sheet-metal table with bent-down tabs for legs to hold the plate an inch above the stove element. Large holes drilled in the table vent the heat which otherwise would pour out around the edge and burn the handles of the tools. Unless you have a cylinder-former for making the ring of $\frac{1}{8}$-inch strap aluminum, you will find it easier to make the table square. Fasten all parts together with pop rivets.

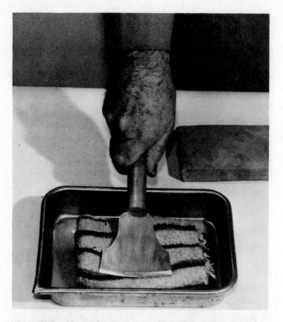

Illus. 250—Heat the lining tool until it "spits" when touched by a drop of water or a wet finger. Then draw it across a wet towel in a pan to lose the excess heat. First one side, then the other. Remove before the hissing stops, and wipe the edge of the pallet on the leather pad in the background.

Illus. 251—Running blind lines on each side of the bands. The flat side of the pallet is toward the band. Slowly roll the pallet across the back of the book. Rub it back and forth a little to make the blind line shiny.

able are brass letters cut one to a shank and provided with a wooden handle. Brass type is also available for use with the lettering pallet. The advantage of brass type is that it is not possible to damage or melt it with the heat provided by the finishing stove. However, brass type is rather expensive, especially for the beginning amateur, and therefore *foundry type* is recommended.

Foundry type has the highest melting point of all type metals. It is composed of 62 per cent lead, 14 per cent tin, and 24 per cent antimony. It is also the hardest, and therefore the most durable, of type metals. It melts at a temperature of 605° F. = 318.33° Celsius. Linotype metal, with which an entire line of type is cast at one time, contains 84 per cent lead, 4 per cent tin, and 12 per cent antimony. Its melting point is 475° F. = 246.1° C.

The monotype machine is usually used to set up composition composed of individual letters.

Illus. 252—Here is how to blind in a thin line on a leather back with a piece of linen sewing thread. Hold the thread as shown and move it briskly back and forth, bearing down with both hands. The pressure and friction "burn" a thin, dark line across the leather.

147

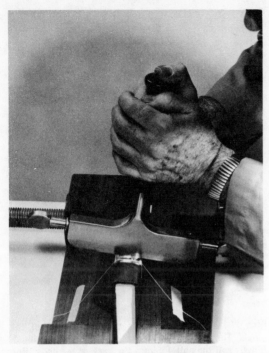

Illus. 253—Easier to handle than gold leaf is gold foil. Simply tape it down to the sides of the book with masking tape, then stretch a guide thread across and tape the ends down to the press as shown. The tapered edge of the lettering pallet allows the type to be seen and guided along the thread. Rock the pallet from side to side as you roll it slowly across the back to ensure even stamping of every letter.

Illus. 254—To stamp a design ornament on the back of a book, clamp the stamp in the single-letter pallet and stamp it through foil taped to the back. Guide the tool with your free hand—although the metal is not blistering hot, it is far from cool. If your fingers are at all sensitive to heat, protect them with a light glove.

Sometimes monotype is sold in fonts, but it is best not to use it where heat is involved, though it is perfectly satisfactory for regular printing. It is composed of 76 per cent lead, 8 per cent tin, and 16 per cent antimony; its melting point is 515° F. = 268.3° C. Pure lead has the highest melting point of all: 621.3° F. = 327.38° C., but in its natural state, lead is too soft for printing purposes and must be alloyed to make it more durable.

APPLYING GOLD LEAF TO THE BOOK. Once the vinegar wash is dry, paint a single coat of glair on the title space and let it dry. Take a little Vaseline or other petroleum jelly on a tuft of cotton and rub it over the glair—this is to make the gold leaf stick when put down.

Rub a little Vaseline on the back of your left hand and touch a twist of cotton to it. Use this to pick up a piece of gold leaf and transfer it to the title space. Breathe gently on it to make it lie flat, then transfer another piece of gold leaf and lay it over the first. Tamp down gently with a piece of dry absorbent cotton (cotton wool).

RUNNING THE TITLE WITH THE PALLET. Stretch a piece of thread across the gold leaf to serve as a stamping guide. Measure the length of the line of type in the pallet and set this length off on the gold, centering it. Make a tick in the gold above the thread to indicate where the title is to start.

Heat the pallet of type, cool to the correct temperature, then roll the pallet across the back of the book, along the guide thread. Progress slowly, tilting the pallet from right to left as you go to ensure all parts of all letters will be impressed. (Illus. 253 shows how to do this with gold foil.)

RUNNING A TITLE WITH SINGLE LETTERS. Lay out the capital letter type required. One by one, grip them in the single-letter pallet and roll a brayer coated with printer's ink over the face. Stamp this letter on the pencilled layout on thin paper. Continue until all the letters have been stamped. This printed version will serve as a guide for stamping the back.

Wash the title space with vinegar water, but do not glair it. When dry, tape the title pattern to the book with masking tape. Heat the letters one by one in the pallet and stamp each one in its proper place on the pattern. Remove the paper and you will find the title blinded in on the back of the book. However, it will be a little blurred because of the thickness of the pattern paper; so go over the title again, a letter at a time. You must exercise care in positioning the type exactly over the previous impression; so, protect your fingers from the hot tool with the thumb and forefinger cut in one piece from an old glove. This procedure will sharpen up the letters.

Take a #0 or #00 pointed red sable brush and carefully pencil in a coat of glair on the bottom of each impression, taking care not to get any on the material outside the letter. When the glair dries, apply a second coat the same way.

Rub a thin film of Vaseline over the letters and lay on the gold leaf. Breathe on it to flatten it, then lay on another layer. The blind letters will be clearly visible through the gold. Go over the title once more with hot type in the single-letter pallet, one letter at a time.

CLEANING OFF THE EXCESS GOLD. In both of the above cases, excess gold can be removed by lightly brushing with a plastic or copper mesh pot cleaner. Take care not to scrape down into the letters and do not try to remove every speck of excess gold this way.

Next take a soft cloth or a Webril Handi-Pad (used by printers, lithographers and photographers owing to its softness and lintless qualities) and dampen it with olive oil. Remove excess oil by squeezing the pad in a paper towel or tissue. With this, gently wipe the title space, taking away the remaining loose gold. Stubborn spots can be picked out with a needle. To remove the oil this procedure leaves on the book, take up a little naphtha (lighter fluid) on a cloth or pad and gently wipe the title space clean.

If you practice gold stamping on waste cover material or old books first, you will experience less difficulty when it comes to running the title across the backbone.

STAMPING WITH GOLD FOIL. Foil is much easier to handle than gold leaf. It comes in rolls (Illus. 243). To run a title with a pallet, all you have to do, in the case of leather, is apply a vinegar wash and let dry (not necessary on artificial leather, buckram, cloth, etc.). Then tape a piece of gold foil to the title space, stretch a guide thread across and roll on the title. If there is more than one line in the title, do not set up more than one line at a time in the pallet, or you will run into trouble. Foil carries its own size with it, so it is not necessary to paint the back with glair. (Illus. 253).

After you have cleaned off the back with naphtha, check the lettering. Whether stamping with the lettering pallet or one letter at a time, it often happens that the gold will not "take" in certain spots. In such cases, paint the ungilded parts with two more coats of glair, then apply Vaseline. Whether you have printed with gold leaf or gold foil, make repairs with gold leaf, two layers on. Reheat the letter involved and carefully restamp.

If you have run the title with a pallet, do not attempt to roll the line of type a second time. All corrections therefore will have to be made with gold leaf as described above, a letter at a time.

If you are printing with imitation gold or colored foil, do not make corrections with gold leaf. You may try the foil by just covering the affected spot, leaving the uncovered part of the letter for a guide. Another way is to touch up the lettering with gold paint on a fine-pointed red sable brush.

Illus. 255—Stamping a title slip to be glued to the back of a book. Tape the title slip to a piece of cardboard with masking tape and tape foil over it. Tape a guide thread on as shown. Guide the pallet into position with your free hand, then press down. When contact is made, place both hands on the handle and rock the pallet in all directions to ensure even stamping.

If you have titled with a colored foil, you can buy a similar color of bronzing powder, available at most paint and art supply shops, and mix it to paint consistency in a few drops of acrylic glossy medium.

If a design or other lettering is to be stamped on the back, it most often goes in the next to lowest panel on the spine (Illus. 254), although some binders run a decorative stamp in the middle of each space set off by the bands.

Foil can also be used to run a picture or abstract design on the front cover of the book. First make the drawing on thin paper, then turn it over on a light box or against a window pane. Attach strips of foil only where there are lines, leaving the open spaces blank. Stick the foil on with masking tape. Then turn the drawing face-side up and tape it to the front cover of the book. Use the electric foil-writing pen to go over the lines and transfer the design to the cover material.

TITLE SLIPS. One way to avoid making mistakes on the spine of the book (and is the method of titling sometimes used in publishers' editions), is to stamp the title on leather or cloth and glue it on.

You can get very thin leather in a variety of colors for title slips. If you prefer, however, to make use of scrap pieces of morocco leather you have on hand, prepare it before stamping. The leather piece should always be somewhat larger than the space it is to fill. The leather has a pronounced grain, and this must be flattened to make a clear, legible title. Soak the leather slip in water for about 5 minutes, until soft and flexible. Blot it dry with a paper towel. Place the slip between waxed paper and pressing boards and give it a hard squeeze in the press. Remove and blot up the water squeezed out. Do this several times, until the grain has been mashed down flat.

Thin the leather from the back with a leather knife and feather the edges. Tape the slip to a piece of cardboard (Illus. 255). Give the leather a vinegar wash and let dry. Tape gold foil over it, and over that a guide thread. Stamp as shown in Illus. 255, taking care to get the type located and lined up in the right place. When the slip is stamped, glue it to the back of the book with Elmer's Glue-All. When dry, run a gold line across the back, above and below the title.

THE GOLD-STAMPING MACHINE. Many problems confront the practitioner with the hand-

150

lettering pallet. Problems of correct temperature, the right amount of pressure, and others, are eliminated with the gold-stamping machine. Rolls of pure gold, imitation gold, and colored foil are used in the machine, the main purpose of which is to stamp names or initials on leather goods. If you are casing in a book, the title can be stamped directly on the case before casing in. Or, title slips of cloth, leather, or paper can be gold stamped and glued to the back of the book. The gold-stamping machine cannot be used to stamp a title directly on a book that has been completely bound.

Illus. 236 shows books with various types of bindings and which have been titled in the different ways discussed above. The flowery-looking book in the foreground is covered with a thin, textured upholstery plastic that is backed with cotton cloth.

Additional Techniques

BINDING WITH A FLEXIBLE COVER. This is not the same as a paperback cover. Bibles, Testaments, books of mathematical tables and other pocket reference books are usually bound with flexible covers.

Leather, imitation leather, or cloth-lined plastic are suitable materials for flexible covers. If a little stiffness is desired, make boards by pasting together several sheets of paper—or you can use extremely light cardboard.

If you are starting from scratch, sew on buried cords and back with the shallowest possible backing groove. Trim the boards to size for a tight joint. Cover, trim out the turn-in when dry, and glue down the board papers.

A cover of morocco or other thick leather requires no boards. Paste the board papers directly to the flesh side of the leather. Where there is no turn-in, the corners are usually rounded, and the leather is allowed to overhang the book all around about ¾ inch.

ROUND-CORNERED COVERS. When re-covering a book with round corners, you will also have to provide the cover with round corners. As mentioned above, a thick leather cover is simply cut round. However, if there is to be a turn-in of the leather, pare the edges all around and turn in the edges upon themselves. Gather each corner in a series of pleats, shaping them with the point of an awl, then pressing the pleats flat. Glue down the board papers, directly to the leather, and press with a sheet of aluminum and waxed paper under each cover.

BIBLES AND TESTAMENTS. Religious books are often the most cherished possession a person can have, not only for the religious significance, but also because the book is usually a gift from some beloved person.

Except for such repairs as have been treated in Chapter 15 and re-covering as noted above, shun all such work by recommending the services of a professional bookbinder. He is fully equipped with the right tools and the know-how required to restore such books. Most Bibles are printed on very thin paper, and are difficult to sew. Also, the margins are so narrow that only a whisper may be trimmed off, if any. If the edges are trimmed at all, the corners will have to be rounded again, requiring the use of a corner-rounding machine. If the edges are to be re-gilded, the job is one for the expert gilder—unless you have practiced sufficiently as an amateur to become expert at it. The proper tools and considerable skill are required for edge gilding. And the worst thing you can do is spoil a friend's cherished book under the mistaken impression that you can restore it.

PRESERVING LEATHER BINDINGS. Leather bindings seldom receive proper care, except in those libraries where a staff may be hired to look after such things. Leather gives a book a most prestigious appearance, but it is also the least durable of cover materials if it is not properly protected against aging and rot. It might be mentioned here that leather-bound books should never be taken to the tropics. Only linen buckram is sufficiently durable to resist climatic conditions found in hot, humid areas.

A newly bound book should be treated with a very small amount of white Vaseline rubbed into the leather with the fingers or a soft cloth pad. Apply an extra amount to the hinges, as these require it most. After treatment, place the book in a warm place (about 100° F. = 37.7° C.) for a few hours to encourage penetration of the grease. Leave no greasy residue on the surface of the leather. Repeat the treatment every two or three years and the book will remain continually in good condition.

A neglected leather-covered book that has become old, rotted and worn, with the cover flaking away from dryness, can to some extent be revived by oiling the leather with a preparation made up of 30 per cent anhydrous lanolin, 12 per cent castor oil, 5 per cent pure Japan wax, 3 per cent powdered sodium stearate, and 50 per cent distilled water. Japan wax (or Japan tallow, as it is also called) is a yellowish wax obtained from the berries of the sumac and is used in polishes and textile finishes. The leather turns dark when an oil solution is applied, but the above formula provides the most even coloration (according to the U.S. Dept. of Agriculture Leaflet No. 69, issued in 1930, revised in 1933). Rub the formula into the leather with your fingers or a cloth pad at intervals of an hour or two until the leather is well oiled. Then let stand in a warm place until the next day and polish with a soft cloth.

If the old leather binding is still in good condition—not powdering or flaking away—it may be treated in the same way with a formulation consisting of half and half neat's-foot oil and castor oil.

EDGE COLORING. If you plan to color the edges of a book, do so after trimming the edges and after the book has been rounded and backed. Use waterproof drawing ink in any color desired, or dissolve artists' acrylic tube color in water. Clamp the book tightly to prevent the color from running in between the pages. Usually only the head is colored to protect it from showing accumulated dust. Apply the color in one or two strokes with a sponge and wipe it off immediately with a dry, absorbent rag or paper tissue.

For a mottled coloration, squeeze the sponge nearly dry and try it first on a scrap of paper, dabbing it on with quick strokes. When the sponge stops leaving a spot of solid color and the imprint shows the structure of the sponge, dab it on the edge of the book. A natural sponge is best for this. Allow the color to dry before unclamping.

To speckle the edge with color, place the book under a pressing board and a heavy weight, lying flat. Cover everything except the book edge with newspaper. Dip a bristle paint brush about 2 inches wide into the color and squeeze it almost dry with a paper towel.

Hold a broom handle with one hand, erect in front of the book, and step on the broom straws to hold it down. Rap the brush against the broom handle, on a level with the book. The little color remaining in the brush will spatter and some of it will get on the edge of the book. To get the technique, make a few practice tries before risking the book edge. The broom handle should be about a foot or so from the book.

Or, you can hold a tooth brush a few inches away from the edge (covering all except the surface you want to spatter) and then draw your thumb slowly across the bristles to cause the spatter.

If you want, you can spatter a little of one color, then a little of another, using a different brush. Two or three colors can be applied in this manner for a varied effect.

EDGE GILDING. In some cases, where the value of the book and its binding warrant it, the book edges can be gilded. Often, only the head is gilded, as this is the edge that tends to collect dust. If all three edges are to be gilded, the gilder treats the fore edge first, and then the head and tail in either order.

Gild the edges immediately after trimming them, while the cut surface is still fresh and clean. Place the book between heavy cardboards, hardboards, or a pair of plywood cutting boards, their edges even with the edge to be gilded. Clamp the book in the lying press or a bench press and apply sufficient pressure close to the edge to make it solid so that it won't absorb the fluid glair applied.

To give the gilded edge greater brilliance, treat it first to a coating of bole, which is any one of a number of iron oxide pigments available under various names, such as red chalk, ruddle, red ochre, Armenian bole (a bright red), bole Armoniac, oriental bole, red bole, terra Lemnia, terra pozzuoli, terra rosa, terra sigillata, and Venice or Venetian red. Venetian red is the name most commonly found on the listings of pigment dealers. Do not use Bohemian bole as it is yellow.

Other iron oxides may also be used instead of bole, such as the pigment called English red, also known as colcothar, madder red, Mars red, Prussian red, angel red, Coromandel and Tuscany.

The bole is used in the form of a finely ground pigment-powder.

To make an edge-gilding size, separate the yolk from the white of an egg, then transfer about two teaspoonfuls of the white to a half a cup of water and beat with a fork until well amalgamated. Let stand overnight, then strain before use. If you are using blood or egg albumen in dried crystal form, stir a teaspoonful of the crystals into $\frac{1}{3}$ cup of water, let stand overnight and strain. Don't add vinegar to either formula.

The first step is to scrape the edge with a scraper that has a rounded edge. At head or tail, scrape with the back of the book toward you. In any case, scrape by pushing the scraper away, never drawing it toward you. When the edge has been scraped smooth, rub lightly with 6/0 cabinet paper.

Take out a small quantity of the glair and put it into a sauce dish. Add enough of the powdered bole to make a smooth paste. Dip a wad of absorbent cotton or Webril Handi-Pad into the bole, and apply the color to the edge by gentle rubbing. If you plan to gild only the head, take care not to get any bole on the fore edge. Let the bole dry, then polish it down with a stiff brush or piece of chamois skin (wash leather) until you have produced a smooth, evenly colored surface.

Dust the gold cushion with pumice and knock off the excess by rapping the edge of the cushion against the table. Wipe both sides of the gold knife on the cushion to free it of grease, and wipe it clean with a Kleenex. Transfer a sheet of gold to the cushion and cut it into strips of suitable width.

With an oil-painters' flat, soft-bristled brush about an inch wide, brush edge-gilding glair over the surface of bole, taking care not to slop it over on the fore edge. Before it dries, transfer the gold strips to the glaired surface by means of a strip of paper. Touch one edge of the gold to the glair to adhere it, then withdraw the paper, allowing the leaf to drop into place. Cover the entire edge with gold leaf, then leave it for an hour or two to dry.

To produce a brilliant surface, the gold must be polished with an agate or bloodstone burnisher. First cover the edge with a piece of paper and work the burnisher lightly over the gold to adhere it without tearing it loose in spots. The face of the paper can be waxed to make the burnisher slide more easily. Then remove the paper and continue to burnish lightly, first applying a little bit of beeswax to the gold surface. As the gold becomes more and more firmly adhered, apply heavier and heavier pressure to the burnisher. Move the burnisher back and forth across the edge of the book, not lengthwise.

After gilding, the book is rounded and backed and forwarding continues in the usual way as described elsewhere.

15. Book Repairs

Books, particularly school books, are subject to all kinds of abuse and suffer various damage, including torn or wrinkled pages, ripped or stained covers and broken boards. Some repairs are easily and quickly made; others take more time and trouble. But in no case should a book simply in need of repair be submitted to the entire rebinding process unless there is a particular reason for doing so.

WRINKLED PAGES. Large, heavy dictionaries, encyclopedias, and so on, are particularly prone to wrinkled pages, especially those printed on thin India paper. To remove the wrinkles and flatten the leaf, lay a sheet of white blotter or other soft, clean paper under the leaf and iron the wrinkles out with an electric iron. Stubborn wrinkles may be damped with a damp cloth, then ironed. Where wrinkles continually recur, the page should be ironed flat once and for all, a piece of waxed paper placed under it, and the surface brushed all over with a thin coat of mending paste (see page 157). Cover the page with thin tissue or cheesecloth (muslin), lay waxed paper on top, close the book and press until dry.

DOG-EARED PAGES. The deplorable practice of turning over the corner of a page to mark one's place is an act we have all been guilty of at one time or another. A corner that has only been turned over for a short time can often be dampened and ironed out as described above. However, when the fibres of the paper have been broken along the fold, more rigorous methods must be employed.

Sometimes repainting with size works. Dissolve $\frac{1}{8}$ teaspoonful of rabbit-skin glue or plain, unflavored gelatine in about $1\frac{1}{2}$ teaspoonfuls of hot water. Brush this size into the crease on both sides of the leaf, place waxed paper on both sides, and leave the book under a board and a weight to dry.

MENDING A TORN PAGE. For an ordinary tear up to several inches long, treat as follows: Place waxed paper under the torn sheet and a piece of lens tissue, coffee-filter paper, wiping tissue, or other soft, thin, fibrous paper on top of the waxed paper. Separate the torn edges and apply mending paste (page 157) with a small, pointed, red sable brush to the *edges* only—not the surface of the leaf. Lay the torn edges together upon the fibrous sheet underlaying it, adjusting the tear until an accurate fit can be made. Lay a second sheet of tissue over the tear and, on top of that, a sheet of waxed paper. Close the book and press under heavy pressure until the next day.

Upon removing the book from the press, take away the waxed paper sheets, then carefully tear away the tissue on each side of the leaf, which will be stuck along the line of the tear. Some fibres will be left behind, stuck to the page, and you can remove these by careful rubbing with a pencil eraser.

If the tear was a reasonably clean one and you have done a neat job of fitting the edges together, you will scarcely be able to tell that the leaf was ever torn.

TORN-OUT PAGES OR JAGGED TEARS. Where a leaf has been torn entirely out of a book, or where the tear is long, rough, and jagged, place a sheet of waxed paper under it and assemble the torn pieces as accurately as possible on it. Cut a piece of lens tissue or similar fibrous paper as large as the page, or, at least, large enough to cover the damaged area. Brush a thin coat of paste over the entire page (or the entire area to be covered by the tissue). Lay the tissue down and rub it gently in place, then turn the leaf over on a second sheet of waxed paper. Brush paste over the page as before and place another sheet of tissue over the reverse side of the damaged area. Close the book and press at least until the next day, or until the paste is dry. The tissue is not to be removed, as it is pasted down all over, and the page can be easily read through it, as it is practically invisible.

In extreme cases, where the page is not only torn out or nearly so, but is also badly wrinkled and crushed, first iron the page out as flat as possible. Then repair the page as described in the paragraph above except, instead of tissue, line the surface of the sheet with a wide-mesh cloth such as tarlatan or starched cheesecloth (muslin in England). Press the repaired leaf between sheets of waxed paper until dry.

CLEANING PAGES. Ordinary soil, fingerprints, etc., can often be removed by gentle rubbing with the so-called "dry cleaner" eraser—a block of yellowish gum rubber available at art supply shops. From the same source, you can obtain a "kneaded eraser," which is also good for removing smudges and other surface soil, such as pencils marks.

Also among art supplies is to be found the newer vinyl eraser as well as the vinyl cleaning pad, both much used by draughtsmen for cleaning up drawings. The pad is a powdered form of the vinyl eraser, contained in a small bag of woven material.

Ordinary writing ink and ball-point pen ink can be removed by the sparing use of sodium hypochlorite solution (common household bleach), applied with the point of a toothpick. Blot up quickly and apply again. Repeat until the ink has bleached away. The treatment is also effective against the waterproof ink of some felt-tip pens. It is, however, ineffective against others, as well as against India drawing ink. In such cases, try oxalic acid. Dissolve a few crystals in a small quantity of water and treat as above.

DIRTY COVERS. Books bound in buckram or book cloth can usually be wiped clean with a damp rag, as these materials are loaded with a waterproof, plastic filler. A damp rag will also clean a textile cover that has been treated with Scotchgard. Let the cleaned area dry, then spray with another application of Scotchgard.

THE BOARDS—WORN OR DAMAGED CORNERS. The corners of the boards often suffer when a book is knocked about or used excessively.

When the corners become soft, thickened, and mushy, carefully pull back the cover material (it releases quite easily from the board) and saturate the corner with hard glue—hot glue or cold liquid glue. If the plies are separated, glue in between them, glue the cover material back in place and press with a sheet of flashing aluminum covered with waxed paper under the board.

If the cover material is worn so that the board is exposed, make new corners, as for a half binding, and glue them on. Or, cut a strip of cover material and glue it along the entire fore edge of each board. When the glue has dried, trim out the excess turn-in to the edge of the existing board paper. If the board paper is damaged in the process, cut a new one and glue it in.

TORN, WORN OR DAMAGED SPINE OR HINGES. This includes the area of cover material from the back edge of the front board to the back edge of the end board. Tears often develop in the hinges from much opening of a book—especially dictionaries. The tear in the cover usually starts toward the head, but the tail end of the hinge soon starts to tear also. Self-adhering cloth tape is only an expedient at best and does nothing for the appearance of the book.

In such a case, examine the endpapers and the backing cloth or super. If these are still sound, cut the cover down the back edge of both boards and remove the spine. Make a new spine, preferably of buckram. Either make a three-part hollow back and glue it to the back of the sections, or glue a loose hollow to the new cover. The cover material should be wide enough to overlap the boards by an inch on each side. Mark where the cloth is to come, then brush the cloth with Elmer's Glue-All and apply it as you would the back of a quarter binding. Slit the endpapers to allow for the turn-in under the back of the book. Press between grooving boards, with an aluminum sheet under each board, until the glue dries.

If the original spine is undamaged, you can trim it down and glue it to the back of the new spine. If even just the title area is still in good shape, you can trim that down and glue it on.

Otherwise, retitle the book by one of the methods described in Chapter 14.

WORN-OUT COVER. If the cover is badly worn and soiled all over, yet the endpapers and backing cloth are sound, the only remedy is to recover. Strip the old cover material off the boards and scrape off the old board papers. Tear off the flyleaf of the previous endpapers. Make new, folded-sheet endpapers and tip them on, then recover the book in any style and with any material desired. Complete the job by trimming out the turn-in and pasting down the board papers.

TORN BACKING CLOTH. If the hinge of super or backing cloth is torn and rotted, it must be replaced. Strip the boards of the cover material and board papers and tear off the old flyleaves. Clamp the book and paste the back to soften the old glue. Scrape off the old backing material down to the section folds. Let dry, then reglue and rub down a new super hinge (and headbands if desired).

Make folded endpapers and tip them to the book, then board and cover the book as described in preceding chapters.

If the original cover material is in good shape, you can remove both covers and the spine in the form of the original case. Rework the book as described above, then case it in with the original case.

ENDPAPERS TORN AT THE FOLD. When endpapers tear at the fold, the book becomes loose and is quickly subject to further damage. Repair the torn endpaper with a strip of super pasted along the hinge, half on the flyleaf and half on the board paper. Over this paste a strip of paper. Close the board carefully on waxed paper and press until the repaired hinge is dry.

REBOARDING. Where the boards are badly damaged, the whole case will have to be removed and discarded. Examine the backing and sewing. If these are sound, tear out the old flyleaves, tip on new endpapers and either case in with a new case or board and cover.

Adhesives

GLUE. Hot glue is available in the form of beads or crystals and it is called "ground glue." The best is hide glue, though so-called "animal glue," which is made of bones as well as hides, can also be used.

Soak 4 oz. by weight (113.399 grams) of dry glue in 4 fluid ounces (118.29 cc) of water for several hours until entirely soaked up by the glue. Stir up the gelatinous cake and add a similar quantity more of water. If you have an automatic electric glue pot, you can both soak and cook the glue in the container that goes with the glue pot. (You should have two containers, one for hard glue, one for flexible glue.) Plug in the pot and let the glue cook at least 2 hours—the automatic feature of the pot will keep the glue at the correct temperature.

If you are using an old-fashioned glue pot with a water jacket, or have put the glue in a tin can in a pan of water heating over a flame or electric element (turned to LOW), keep a cooking thermometer immersed in the glue and do not let the temperature of the glue rise above 150° F. (66.5° C.) or it will lose its strength. Do not let the water pan go dry or you will burn the glue.

After 2 hours, test the cooked glue by lifting it on a stirring stick. It should run off quickly and easily, but not be watery. If it is watery, keep on cooking until it thickens a bit. If too thick, add a little hot water.

This glue is called *hard* glue, because it hardens on setting and, if bent, will crack or break. You can make your own *flexible* glue from the same ground glue as above. When cooked, add 4 tablespoonfuls of glycerin to the given amount and stir it in well. Differentiate the pots containing the different glues by marking with an H or an F, using a felt-tip pen.

If you are using cold, liquid hide glue, pour some into a separate container and add $\frac{1}{2}$ to 1 teaspoonful of glycerin for each fluid ounce (29.57 cc) of glue and stir it in thoroughly. The more glycerin you use, the more flexible the glue.

PASTE. Prepared wheat flour paste powder can be obtained from a wallpaper store. Mix what you need by adding water in accordance with the directions on the package.

HOME-MADE FLOUR-AND-WATER PASTE. To ½ cup wheat flour, add 5 level teaspoonfuls of powdered alum and stir together. Measure out 2 cups of water. Add a little water to the flour-alum mixture and stir until smooth and fluid; then, add the rest of the water, stir, and place over medium heat. Cook with constant stirring until the mixture boils. Reduce the heat and continue cooking for 5 minutes, continuing to stir. When cooked, stir in ⅛ teaspoonful of oil of cloves for a preservative and pour the paste into a clean jar that has been rinsed with boiling water and let dry. Cool before using.

MENDING PASTE FOR BOOK REPAIR. Take 1 tablespoonful of rice flour, 2 tablespoonfuls of corn starch, ½ teaspoonful of powdered alum. Stir 3 fluid ounces (88.7 cc) of water into the mixture. (You can buy rice flour at a health food store. However, wheat flour and laundry starch can be substituted in the formula.)

Warm the mixture in a pan over a slow heat with constant stirring until it thickens into a pasty mass. It is not necessary to cook the paste after it has thickened. Remove from the heat, stir in a few drops of oil of cloves, and transfer to a clean, scalded glass jar for future use. Cool before using.

Appendix

Book Sizes

The system of denoting book sizes is very old. It was based on the size of sheet prevailing at the time, and the size into which it was folded to make each section or signature. There is always an even number of pages to a section, the sheet being folded so as to produce 4, 8, 12, 16, 24, 32, 48, 64 pages, and so on. (Only one half as many leaves as pages, since a leaf, printed on both sides, consists of 2 pages.) The tables below give information for certain sizes of modern sheets, though actual page sizes may be a little smaller than the figures given, since the book is trimmed an undetermined amount at head, tail and fore edge. British sheet sizes also differ somewhat from the American, and the page sizes therefore will also differ a little.

TABLE I

SIZE NAME w/abbr. and symbol	TIMES SHEET FOLDED	LEAVES TO SHEET	PAGES TO SHEET	PAGE SIZE IN INCHES
royal folio (fo, or f)	1	2	4	$20 \times 12\frac{1}{2}$
royal quarto (4to, 4°)	2	4	8	$12\frac{1}{2} \times 10$
royal octavo (8vo, 8°)	3	8	16	$10 \times 6\frac{1}{4}$
royal sixteenmo (16mo, 16°)	4	16	32	$6\frac{1}{4} \times 5$
royal thirty-twomo (32mo, 32°)	5	32	64	$5 \times 3\frac{1}{8}$
royal sixty-fourmo (64mo, 64°)	6	64	128	$3\frac{1}{8} \times 2\frac{1}{2}$
medium folio	1	2	4	$18 \times 11\frac{1}{2}$
medium quarto	2	4	8	$11\frac{1}{2} \times 9$
medium octavo	3	8	16	$9 \times 5\frac{3}{4}$
medium sixteenmo	4	16	32	$5\frac{3}{4} \times 4\frac{1}{2}$
medium thirty-twomo	5	32	64	$4\frac{1}{2} \times 2\frac{7}{8}$
medium sixty-fourmo	6	64	128	$2\frac{7}{8} \times 2\frac{1}{4}$
crown folio	1	2	4	15×10
crown quarto	2	4	8	$10 \times 7\frac{1}{2}$
crown octavo	3	8	16	$7\frac{1}{2} \times 5$
crown sixteenmo	4	16	32	$5 \times 3\frac{3}{4}$
crown thirty-twomo	5	32	64	$3\frac{3}{4} \times 2\frac{1}{2}$
crown sixty-fourmo	6	64	128	$2\frac{1}{2} \times 1\frac{7}{8}$

TABLE II

SIZE NAME	SCALE OF THE AMERICAN LIBRARY ASSOCIATION SYMBOL	OUTSIDE HEIGHT	SIZE OF FRONT COVER
folio (fo or f)	F	over 30 cm	12×19
quarto (4to, 4°)	Q	25–30 cm	$9\frac{1}{2} \times 12$
octavo (8vo, 8°)	O	20–25 cm	6×9
imperial octavo	O		$8\frac{1}{4} \times 11\frac{1}{2}$
super octavo	O		7×11
royal octavo	O		$6\frac{1}{2} \times 10$
medium octavo	O		$6\frac{3}{8} \times 9\frac{1}{4}$
crown octavo	O		$5\frac{3}{4} \times 8$
duodecimo (12mo, 12°)	D	17.5–20 cm	$5 \times 7\frac{3}{8}$
duodecimo (large)	D	17.5–20 cm	$5\frac{1}{2} \times 7\frac{1}{2}$
sextodecimo (16mo, 16°)	S	15–17.5 cm	$4 \times 6\frac{3}{4}$
octodecimo (18mo, 18°)	T	12.5–15 cm	$4 \times 6\frac{1}{2}$
trigesimo-secundo (32mo, 32°)	Tt	10–12.5 cm	$3\frac{1}{2} \times 5\frac{1}{2}$
quadragesimo-octavo (48mo, 48°)	Fe	7.5–10 cm	$2\frac{1}{2} \times 4$
sexagesimo-quarto (64mo, 64°)	Sf	less than 7.5 cm	2×3

NOTE: Above tables from "Webster's Third New International Dictionary, 1971."

Sources of Supply in the United States

Suppliers to the bookbinding trade:
Gane Bros. & Lane, Inc.
1400 Greenleaf Ave.
Elk Grove Village, Ill. 60607
(Chicago area)

with branches at:
4115 Forest Park Blvd.
St. Louis, Mo. 63108

161 MacQuesten Pky. So.
Mt. Vernon, New York 10550
(New York City area)

1511 Prudential Drive
Dallas, Texas 75235

218 Littlefield Avenue
South San Francisco, Calif. 94080

150 Mendel Drive, S.W.
Atlanta, Georgia 30336

4697 East 48th Street
Vernon, California 90058
(Los Angeles area)

Bookbinding tools, supplies, general hobby supplies:
The Craftool Co., Inc.
1421 W. 240th Street
Harbor City, Calif. 90710

Henry Westphal & Co.
4 East 32nd Street
New York, N.Y. 10016

The W. O. Hickok Mfg. Co.
Ninth and Cumberland Streets
Harrisburg, Pennsylvania 17105

Non-warping paste and other adhesives:
S. & W. Framing Supplies, Inc.
1845 Highland Avenue
New Hyde Park, New York 11040

Liquid and dry-ground hide glue:
Craftsman Wood Service Co.
2727 South Mary Street
Chicago, Ill. 60608
(Request catalog)

Planatol BB adhesive:
In the U.S.:
Gane Bros. & Lane, Inc.

European address:
Planatolwerk W. Hesselmann,
82 Rosenheim, West Germany

Hemp and linen twine:
Albert Constantine and Son, Inc.
2050 Eastchester Road,
Bronx, New York 10461

Hard-to-find tools, mallets, knives, etc.:
Brookstone Company
119 Brookstone Bldg.
Peterborough, New Hampshire 03458
(Catalog sent free on request)

Printing presses, type, etc.:
The Kelsey Company
Meriden, Connecticut 06450

Acme Type
732 Federal
Chicago, Ill. 60605
(Catalog $1, refundable)

Type foundry, Pacific Coast:
Mackenzie & Harris, Inc.
460 Bryant Street
San Francisco, Calif. 94107
(Type catalog on request)

Other sources of bookbinding supplies:
Basic Crafts Co.
312 East 23rd Street
New York, N.Y. 10010

Paxton Equipment Supply
7401 South Pulaski Road
Chicago, Illinois 60629

A. I. Friedman, Inc.
25 West 45th Street
New York, N.Y. 10036

Sources of Supply in the United Kingdom

Marbled paper, finishing stoves

Cefmor-Brehmer Ltd
Tarif Road
London, N.17

Dryad Handicrafts
Northgates
Leicester

Douglas Cockerell & Son Ltd.
Riversdale
Grantchester, Cambridge

Book cloth
Thomas Goodall & Co. Ltd.
18 St. Swithins Lane
London, E.C.4

Leather, supplies, equipment
J. Hewit & Sons Ltd.
97 St. John Street,
London, E.C.1
and
125 High Street,
Edinburgh 1

Millboard and other board materials
Jackson's Millboard and Fibre Co Ltd.
Bourne End, Bucks

Handmade and decorative papers
T. N. Lawrence & Sons
2 Bleeding Heart Yard
Greville Street,
London, E.C.1

Leather
H. Band & Co. Ltd.
Brent Way,
High Street,
Brentford, Middlesex

G. W. Russel & Sons Ltd.
The Grange, Bermondsey
London, S.E.1

Paper and strawboard
Spicer-Cowan Ltd.
28-42 Banner Street
London, E.C.1.

Gold leaf and foil, handle letters and brass type
George M. Whiley Ltd.
Victoria Road,
South Ruislip, Middlesex

Adhesives
Croid
Imperial House
15 Kingsway
London, W.C.2

Index